Exploring Florida's
Emerald Coast

Florida A&M University, Tallahassee
Florida Atlantic University, Boca Raton
Florida Gulf Coast University, Ft. Myers
Florida International University, Miami
Florida State University, Tallahassee
New College of Florida, Sarasota
University of Central Florida, Orlando
University of Florida, Gainesville
University of North Florida, Jacksonville
University of South Florida, Tampa
University of West Florida, Pensacola

JEAN LUFKIN BOULER

Exploring Florida's

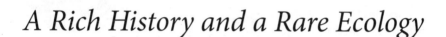

Emerald Coast

A Rich History and a Rare Ecology

Enjoy the beach !

Jean Lufkin Bouler

UNIVERSITY PRESS OF FLORIDA

Gainesville · Tallahassee · Tampa · Boca Raton · Pensacola · Orlando · Miami · Jacksonville · Ft. Myers · Sarasota

Copyright 2007 by Jean Lufkin Bouler
Printed in the United States of America on recycled, acid-free paper
12 11 10 09 08 07   6 5 4 3 2 1
A record of cataloging-in-publication data is available from
the Library of Congress.
ISBN 978-0-8130-3086-9

The University Press of Florida is the scholarly publishing agency for the State
University System of Florida, comprising Florida A&M University, Florida
Atlantic University, Florida Gulf Coast University, Florida International
University, Florida State University, New College of Florida, University of
Central Florida, University of Florida, University of North Florida, University
of South Florida, and University of West Florida.

University Press of Florida
15 Northwest 15th Street
Gainesville, FL 32611-2079
http://www.upf.com

For my mother and father

Contents

I began spending summer vacations on the Emerald Coast twenty-five years ago and over the years became curious about the land and its past. I discovered that this stretch of beach in northwest Florida between Pensacola and Panama City, which used to be called the "Redneck Riviera," has a rich history and a rare ecology.

Along the way I became acquainted with Sam Story, an Indian chief who befriended early Scots settlers; Billy Bowlegs, a legendary pirate who remains a mystery; and Leonard Destin, founder of a fishing tradition. I learned that Wallis Simpson cruised local waters before she married the Duke of Windsor who gave up the British throne. I read about William Lazarus discovering one of the most important relics ever found in the Southeast in a mound at Fort Walton Beach.

This coastal area has been home to man since prehistoric times. Since the 1800s archaeologists have dug up relics that tell how early man lived, with some finds rewriting the history books.

Though the Emerald Coast is now one of the most popular destinations in Florida, tracts of preserved nature areas offer a close-up view of undisturbed coastal wildlife. Dunes and Western Lake at Grayton Beach contrast sharply with wetlands and desertlike scrub at Rocky Bayou.

An underground limestone foundation that resembles Swiss cheese results in springs that bubble to the surface. And beneath the ocean, Desoto Canyon slices through the Gulf floor, bringing deep water close to Destin, which is why the fishing is so good here.

In libraries from Texas to Washington, D.C., I discovered books that tell the tales of the people and the land. In century-old books so brittle I was afraid the pages would crack, writers, naturalists, and adventurers from Chicago, New York, and Boston and from Florida, Georgia, and Alabama told what they saw and whom they met while exploring this coast. In other books so new their bindings were still stiff, scholars and scientists pulled together decades of research using fiber-optics, computers, and artifacts in museums in England, France, and Spain.

Accounts by authors ranging from a reporter traveling through the area after the Civil War to an archaeologist who kept meticulous notes have been published by national houses such as Scribners and Lippincott or by small companies whose printings have kept town histories alive. I was thrilled to find a book by an adventurer who described meeting Leonard Destin and was delighted to read about the details of pioneer life as told by a settler's descendent.

I hope *Exploring Florida's Emerald Coast* will join these earlier works in sharing the unique features of the land and revealing the special stories of its people so that both might be preserved.

Acknowledgments

This book would not have been possible without the resources of the Birmingham Public Library's Southern History Department. The collection of Florida books there was invaluable in my search for information about the history and ecology of the Emerald Coast region. In particular, no history of the Emerald Coast would be complete without the detail in the *History of Walton County*, which I discovered in the department's collection.

Kathryn Ziewitz and Faith Eidse provided numerous beneficial suggestions to improve the manuscript.

Especially helpful were Gail Lynn Meyer of the Indian Temple Mound Museum in Fort Walton Beach and Chris LaRoche of the Heritage Museum of Northwest Florida. Dean DeBolt, Katrina King, and Mike Malone of the University of West Florida Special Collections Department helped provide material from their library. Donald Ware of the Choctawhatchee Audubon Society gladly shared his knowledge. Chick Huettel, who owns Bayou Arts and Antiques and is a member of the area historical society, gave much of his time to reading the manuscript.

The Florida Memory Project, which provided photographs, was a valuable resource. Carol Williams of the Williams' Gallery in Defuniak Springs, Florida, was also helpful.

I am grateful to Meredith Morris-Babb, director of the University Press of Florida, for having faith in the project and to John Byram, editor-in-chief, for seeing it through to publication.

My husband, Nick, was as interested in the creation of the book as if it had been his own. I am fortunate that he is a talented writer and editor.

Exploring Florida's
Emerald Coast

1. Pieces of the Past

Curiosity pulled Colonel William Lazarus into a world far from the supersonic jets and modern technology of Eglin Air Force Base where he was chief civilian scientific adviser. A slim figure with light gray hair and dark-rimmed glasses, he resembled Mr. Rogers, with his gentle smile, bow tie, and cardigan. He often enjoyed smoking a pipe.

Lazarus yearned to know how early natives lived on the Emerald Coast before Columbus discovered America, before paper and pencil, before wars, worship, and daily life were recorded as history. With passion and patience, he spent seven years in the 1950s carefully probing into a mound of earth five feet tall and twenty-five feet in diameter that had been built by prehistoric peoples.[1]

His diligence paid off. He found a host of artifacts that revealed a mysterious world. But there was one discovery that surpassed all the others. In a drama that John Grisham could spin into a best seller, the hunt for remnants of early civilizations led Lazarus to an unusual ceramic figure now considered to be one of the most important ever found in the Southeast and often prominently featured in archaeology books. He found pieces scattered in the mound that, when glued together, formed a four-legged hunchback figure.[2] As in a compelling novel, throughout his work Lazarus struggled to overcome numerous obstacles, conquering most.

His discoveries added to a wealth of artifacts that other archaeologists had unearthed over decades on the Emerald Coast, where prehistoric peoples had lived for at least twelve thousand years. Lazarus and his wife, Yulee, established the Indian Temple Mound Museum to showcase the significant discoveries. The museum now houses more than ten thousand artifacts found by Lazarus and others within a forty-mile radius.

The museum is nestled near a grand ceremonial mound built between AD 800 and 1400, which is still standing on the Miracle Strip Parkway in Fort Walton Beach and now surrounded by shops and motels. The mound, with a

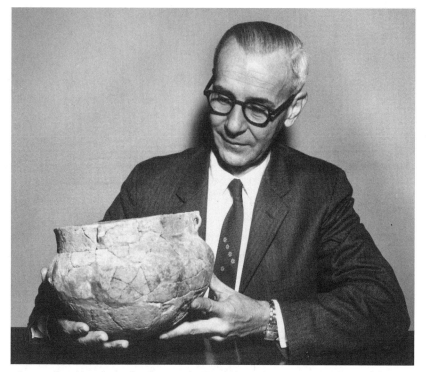

1. Lazarus found hundreds of artifacts on the Emerald Coast. By permission of the Indian Temple Mound Museum, Fort Walton Beach, Fla.

thatched temple replica on top, is a reminder of those early civilizations and has been declared a National Historic Landmark.

Inside the museum, remnants or replicas of fish-bone tools, bowls, and other artifacts of everyday life are arranged in creative displays to show how humans lived here beginning thousands of years ago through more modern times. Hundreds of other artifacts line shallow drawers built into closets.

Lazarus knew that the quest for prehistoric remnants, which are found in such abundance here, had drawn archaeologists to this coast since the 1880s. He eagerly studied their work.

One of the earliest of these researchers was Sylvanus T. Walker, who, by 1879, began collecting bird skins and other specimens for the Smithsonian Institution while living in the Tampa Bay area. Born in Alabama in 1837, Walker moved to the town of Milton and trekked across the Emerald Coast, taking meticulous notes that detailed the location of prehistoric mounds.

Walker described the archaeological bonanza he found: "In the fields, the crops are growing in beds of shell, and the furrows are full of broken pottery and fragments of clay figures." His work was published in the 1883 Smithsonian Institution annual report, a national publication studied by scientists throughout the country. That report was his last one, however, for he became the editor of the *Santa Rosa News* and served as school superintendent. Other archaeologists who picked up the trail to that distant past would study Walker's findings for more than a century.[3]

In the early 1900s, Clarence Bloomfield Moore, a wealthy Pennsylvanian, traveled throughout the Emerald Coast and unearthed hundreds of artifacts. He reported on the Fort Walton Beach site Lazarus later excavated, called Buck Mound, as well as many others. Moore and another archaeologist who followed, Gordon Willey, came to be among the most acclaimed in the country.

Moore discovered twenty-one sites at Fort Walton, Rocky Bayou, Point Washington, and the inlets around Choctawhatchee Bay. The mounds he located were from two to twelve feet high and up to eighty feet in diameter. Some were burial sites; others were piles of clam and oyster shells. He also examined the temple mound where the museum is today.[4]

At St. Andrews Bay, near present-day Panama City, Moore excavated mounds that historians believe were mostly made of oyster shells and other refuse left by inland tribes who came to the coast for seafood. One such pile, at West Bay, was huge, measuring thirty feet tall and spanning fifteen acres.

Information about Moore's life is sketchy. Much of what is known was gathered by Vernon James Knight Jr., an anthropology professor at the University of Alabama and the curator of southeastern archaeology with the Alabama Museum of Natural History. Knight wrote a book about the famed Moundville site in Alabama that had been excavated by Moore. After graduating from Harvard University at the age of twenty-seven Moore became president of the family business in Philadelphia, the Jessup and Moore Paper Company, which he inherited when his father died. He had an adventurous streak. After traveling the world from Asia to the Amazon, he began to spend winters in warm Florida, where historians believe he worked at excavation sites with the curator of Harvard's Peabody Museum.

Moore developed a passion for unearthing intriguing artifacts, a passion that led him to the Emerald Coast. At age forty-seven, Moore decided to devote himself to archaeology full-time. Each year he took a train south from Philadelphia to Florida, then boarded his boat, the *Gopher,* with a crew of eighteen men. They dug into mounds along the Emerald Coast, uncovering hundreds of pottery pieces. After several months, he would take the train back to Philadelphia, where he photographed and studied the artifacts, then wrote about what he had found.

The Academy of Natural Sciences of Philadelphia, which had sponsored some of his expeditions, exhibited the artifacts and published his papers. His annual ritual lasted for more than twenty-five years, taking him throughout the Southeast excavating various sites. His work made him a leading authority on archaeology in the region, while his zealous unearthing of remains—destroying sites in the process—has made him perhaps the most controversial of the region's researchers.[5]

Years later, the famed archaeologist Gordon Willey embarked on an adventure that took him to the Emerald Coast when he was twenty-five years old and resulted in a celebrated book that earned him immediate acclaim. Born in 1913 in Chariton, Iowa, Willey received his undergraduate degree from the University of Arizona and doctorate from Columbia University. In 1938, he traveled to northwest Florida, where he analyzed publications by Moore and others, along with various collections and field notes, to produce a detailed examination of archaeology in the state from the Panhandle to the lower western coast.[6]

In the summer of 1940, Willey and a colleague, Richard Woodbury, studied maps Moore had made and used them to travel to excavation sites. The project was harrowing at times. Willey wrote in his journal entry for June 23 that, while trying to find sites at Hogtown Bayou and Point Washington, their station wagon got so mired in muck that it sealed the doors shut. Woodbury raced the motor, but the station wagon just sank lower. Water poured into the vehicle. The sun began to sink in the sky as the motor stalled. A water moccasin got tangled in the steering column. "We whipped out our pocket knives and were preparing to cut a hole through the top of the roof to escape a horrible death when the wagon began to rise slowly out of the treacherous 'great dank,'" Willey wrote. "Some mysterious pressure raised us about two feet, enough for the right front window to be opened and for us to half crawl, half swim out."[7]

Although in that adventure they were unable to find the cemetery that

2. Lazarus makes field notes at Buck Mound. By permission of the Indian Temple Mound Museum, Fort Walton Beach, Fla.

they were looking for, they did find many other sites. In his book *Archeology of the Florida Gulf Coast,* first published by the Smithsonian Institution in 1949, he describes a Hogtown Bayou cemetery that had been excavated by Moore. There were more than a hundred burials. Vessels had been placed over the skulls. Artifacts included pottery, lance blades, knives, beads, and a copper pendant.

Willey's book was hailed from the start as a classic. The year after the book was first published, Willey became a professor at Harvard, where he taught for thirty-six years and served as curator of anthropology at the Harvard Peabody Museum. Nearly fifty years later, the book, reprinted by the University Press of Florida, is still kept handy for reference by field archaeologists. When Willey died in 2002, the *Harvard University Gazette* called him the premier American archaeologist of the second half of the twentieth century.

William Lazarus successfully followed in the footsteps of Moore and Willey. Before breaking ground at Buck Mound in March 1958, Lazarus sketched the contours of the mound and then drew a diagram dividing it into twenty-four sections of five-foot squares. Lazarus knew the numbered squares would be important to identify excavation areas and to pinpoint artifact finds.[8]

With shovels and trowels, workers gingerly picked into a top layer of hard black muck the mound builders had hauled from a nearby swamp and slathered over the top of the mound. Like prospectors panning for gold, Lazarus and his crew sifted dirt through a screen of quarter-inch mesh looking for any signs of past life.

They found a cremation pit full of shells that had been heated, crushed, and mixed to make concrete, traces of red iron ore on what had apparently been the bases of red-painted totem poles, three-foot-long strips of clay where pottery had been made, and scattered pieces of vessels that had been thrown to the ground in a burial ritual. One of the buried was a young man, about twenty-one years old, whose skeleton showed he had suffered from bone disease.[9]

Discovering these artifacts helped Lazarus and his crew maintain their enthusiasm despite frustrations ranging from fire ants to thunderstorms during eight years of excavating. The work became especially tedious in Pit 17, toward the center of the mound. Roots of a seventy-five-year-old pine seemed to block every stab of the shovel. At each one, the worker had to stop and carefully examine the surrounding dirt for any archaic fragments before hacking through the root with an ax. The crew would soon learn how easy it could be to chop into a priceless artifact.[10]

Despite bees and wasps, as well as the annoying ants, Lazarus continued excavating. Late one afternoon, coming to what must have seemed the thousandth root, a worker fought the urge to hack through the wood. Scraping away the dirt, a small root was uncovered that had grown through a ceramic

3. Lazarus probes excavation pit. By permission of the Indian Temple Mound Museum, Fort Walton Beach, Fla.

leg several inches long. A few inches away, another root pierced the ankle of a ceramic foot.[11]

Lazarus realized the shards were significant. He set up lights so they could keep working into the night. More fragments were unearthed nearby—white, brown, or rosy red, some smaller than a thumbnail. The pieces were soggy from absorbing ground moisture, so he put them on a pedestal in the pit to dry and harden. At midnight, Lazarus called Dr. Charles Fairbanks at Florida State University, an archaeologist involved with the project. Fairbanks said he would be there the next morning.

Lazarus would remember that night for the rest of his life. The workers uncovered more than one hundred pieces. When the parts were glued together, four legs formed the base of a vessel shaped like a hunchback wearing a cape, standing more than a foot tall and about nine inches around.

When Fairbanks arrived, he announced that the figure was spectacular, different from any other pottery found in the Southeast. They would learn

4. The unique Buck Mound burial urn, pieced together from more than one hundred fragments, is often featured in archaeology books. By permission of the Indian Temple Mound Museum, Fort Walton Beach, Fla.

later that the figure was about fifteen hundred years old. However, a critical part was missing—the face.

Lazarus tried to plot where that last fragment would have fallen. On his excavation diagram, he marked which of the twenty-four squares had contained the pieces that had been found. The pattern indicated that the figure likely had been "stabbed" and thrown to the ground and shattered as part of a burial ceremony. Pieces had tumbled down the slope on the south side. The face, then, should be just beyond the base, Lazarus thought. But digging there failed to turn up the missing piece.[12]

Lazarus must have stared at the gaping hole of the faceless urn hundreds of times, wondering what it would look like with the last piece in place. He would revisit his diagram, calculating where the crucial missing piece should have been located.

Over the next few years, his team excavated more sections of the mound. They found stone points and bone tools along with various pottery relics, one in the shape of a turkey, another a male figure. But not the missing piece of the faceless urn. In 1965, seven years after he began excavating Buck Mound, Lazarus died. He still had not found the face.

The next year, workers dug just beyond the mound on the south side, next to Pit 12, where Lazarus had calculated the face would have settled. There, six inches from where Lazarus had searched, buried only as deep as the blade of a shovel, were two objects that at first looked like shallow bowls.[13]

Brushing off the dirt exposed eyes, nose, and mouth—the missing face. Lazarus would be pleased to know that visitors to the Indian Temple Mound Museum can see it today.

Over the years, residents of the area have found precious artifacts by accident. In 1971, while looking over a plot of land where they planned to build a house, Joe Ware and his wife, Inez, found a piece of pottery depicting an eye and nose. Eventually they found sixty pieces that formed a human effigy that had been made sometime between AD 600 and 900. It is one of the most prized pieces at the Indian Temple Mound Museum.

Such findings are especially important because they are all that remain of civilizations that have disappeared. A stroll through the museum reveals interesting details about how those early peoples looked and lived. One display shows that native tribes probably migrated to the Emerald Coast over generations beginning at least twelve thousand years ago to escape glaciers of the north. These first peoples, called Paleo-Indians, were at one time thought to have been Asians who had migrated to North America across a swath of land a thousand miles wide that once connected the two continents at the Bering Strait. But new evidence suggests the first humans might have come from the southern hemisphere and much earlier in time.

A site discovered in Santa Rosa County, north of Pensacola, dates back to at least 9000 BC. It is one of the most significant in the country and is designated on the National Register of Historic Places. A University of West Florida archaeological team located the site along Thomas Creek, a tributary of the Escambia River, in 1983, after amateurs found artifacts in the area.

Scattered across an area more than six miles long and three miles wide were remnants from those early civilizations.[14] Those findings, which include fragments of stone tools made nearly twelve thousand years ago, are rewriting the history books. They indicate that instead of following herds of bison and other game as previously believed, early humans here were able to find enough food to settle in a camp.

They ate nuts and berries from forests and fish and oysters from waterways. Archaeologists have found heaps of oyster shells along the Emerald Coast, indicating this was a main source of food.

The region's early inhabitants efficiently utilized the materials around them. Their lives depended on it. Over the years, they learned how to make fish hooks from bones, spear points from stone, scrapers from claws, and drinking vessels from shells.

Their spears, skillfully made from several materials, were some of the most important devices they made. Tribesmen swung hammerstones to break chunks of chert, a material found in area limestone formations. Using sharp antler horns, they meticulously flaked the chert into points. The points were attached to a piece of ivory from mammoths and fastened to a wooden handle, making a spear. In time these people developed a spear thrower, called an atlatl. A display at the museum shows how the atlatl extended from the arm and increased distance and power when tribesmen threw the spear.[15]

Spear points found in springs indicate that natives crouched beside the watering holes waiting for bison and mammoths. As the animals lowered their massive heads to drink, the natives took careful aim with their spears.

To make utensils, they traded shell for stone from as far away as the Great Lakes. Tribes probably passed material from one camp to another along trade routes that connected various regions.[16] Early peoples especially valued stone because they could use it to make axes or grinders.

The variety of tools found shows that over thousands of years, prehistoric peoples gradually adopted more sophisticated survival techniques. From 8000 to 1000 BC, during the Archaic period, they ventured from settlements established along wetlands to hunt, often camping where food, stone, and other resources could be found. They retooled their weapons for smaller game, chipping shorter, sharper points to kill turkey and deer instead of mammoths and other large animals. They hammered more intricate small stone tools to weave baskets, work hide, or to scrape, slice, chop, and drill. They carved vessels from gourds, large shells, and wood. Tribe members built contraptions called weirs that trapped fish in shallow water near the shore when the tide was high.[17]

Building fires became a crucial skill not only for cooking and warmth, but also for tool and pottery making. These early people could start fires by rotating a pointed dowel in a wooden block, eventually igniting flammable fibers positioned nearby.[18]

As shown at the Indian Temple Mound Museum, these early inhabitants built racks from branches to hold fish and small game that were roasted over the flames. They cooked some foods in a skin bag that was placed in embers. Clay balls about the size of tennis balls, found at Elliott's Point, are thought to have been heated in fires, then put in a pit to cook food.[19] Fire was also used to heat and harden the tips of spears and arrows. Tribe members built canoes by carefully burning the inside of yellow pine logs, fanning flames, and controlling the burning by dabbing wet clay. A similar process created wooden bowls. Inside huts, fires were built to ward off mosquitoes. Burning torches lighted the way for night fishing. Small fires were also important elements in rituals. In a cleansing ceremony, a small fire was built on a mound, where natives drank tea from an adorned bowl.[20]

Another crucial use of fire was in making pottery. About 1170 BC—centuries before construction of the mounds that Moore, Lazarus, and other archaeologists discovered—the early tribes discovered how to make pottery. The native people crushed dried clay and added water as well as Spanish moss to make a doughy substance that was kneaded like bread and formed into vessels. They cut decorations into them with shells, sticks, or feathers and then heated the objects in a fire.

The invention of pottery drastically improved life for prehistoric peoples trying to survive on this coast. The impact was similar to that of electricity on our modern world. Although we take pottery for granted, archaeologists emphasize the importance of the new technology to early peoples. Ceramic bowls, urns, and pots "revolutionized both the storage and the preparation of food."[21] The vessels provided a way to store water and to simmer food by indirect heat over a fire.

Archaeologists and historians treasure pottery because it is one of the few materials that can withstand the disintegrating effects of time. By studying the shapes, designs, and source materials of pottery found along the Emerald

5. The shallow six-sided plate has only been found on the Emerald Coast. By permission of the Indian Temple Mound Museum, Fort Walton Beach, Fla.

Coast, scholars have learned what the ancient peoples and their world looked like—the kind of jewelry they wore, the animals they hunted, the plants picked, games played, and objects worshipped.[22] We can observe innovations in craftsmanship with the pottery as well; over time, the method of making pottery in this area changed as sand was added to the mix and they learned to form shapes by coiling the clay. Bowls, plates, and vessels also have revealed that unlike the peoples in other areas of Florida, various cultures emerged along the Emerald Coast.

Particularly interesting are six-sided plates that are unique to the Emerald Coast and can be seen at the Indian Temple Mound Museum. They might have been used to evaporate seawater for salt, to pass in ceremonies, or to represent a calendar or tribal community house.

As more advanced social and religious practices were adopted, weapons became more sophisticated. Bows and arrows replaced stone-pointed spears by AD 800, in the Woodland period. Historians note that with more efficient methods of getting and cooking food, the tribes had time for other activities, such as mound building and burial rituals. Pottery became more decorative and farming grew more extensive.

During this period, the mound by today's museum in Fort Walton Beach was built. Tribesmen heaped basket after basket full of dirt—some five hundred thousand baskets in all—and packed the soil into a square. On top, they built a thatched-roof temple with a ramp on one side. The mound was used as a central meeting place for religious ceremonies, for political meetings, to mourn the dead, and for public activities.

Burial mounds also have been found. At these sites, some bowls that have been unearthed have holes drilled in them, perhaps to release spirits. Ceramic bottles and dishes found near skeletons were probably buried for use in the afterlife.[23]

These prehistoric peoples pierced themselves extensively. Based on the evidence of artifacts found and early European reports and drawings, they threaded decorative ornaments of fur, bones, and shells through their noses, lips, and ears. They made tattoos by puncturing the skin and rubbing in ocher from iron ore or charcoal dust, covering nearly every inch of their bodies. Bands of shells adorned their arms. One practice—particularly appalling to us in our century—was that of pulling teeth or filing them as a mark of beauty.

6. Local artist Erma Hughes's conception of natives planting a garden. By permission of the Indian Temple Mound Museum, Fort Walton Beach, Fla.

Men slathered bear grease or fish oil over their hair then gathered it into a small knot on top of their heads. Women wore their tresses long and loose until married, then sometimes wore crew cuts or braids. Some shaved their heads, perhaps believing, like the Egyptians, that baldness was the ultimate sign of femininity—or perhaps it was just more practical or cooler in the hot weather.

Warm temperatures for much of the year enabled them to wear little clothing. Women went bare breasted, with Spanish moss, other plant fibers, or deerskin tied around their waists. Men wore strips of fur or plants that looked like a diaper or two aprons. Sometimes they just secured bunches of bark or leaves with a belt. In winter, they wore mantles of fur or feathers draped over one shoulder. They made headdresses of feathers from owls, herons, and other birds. Tribal leaders wore stuffed birds, including the talons, on their heads.

Pieces of the prehistoric past revealed by painstakingly sifting through layers of soil and sand are significant. But many mysteries remain. Despite all their improvements in survival techniques, something went terribly wrong, and these early civilizations vanished. Their fate could have been linked to events unfolding halfway around the world, in the continent of Europe.

Places to Visit

Indian Temple Mound Museum, 139 SE Miracle Strip Parkway, Fort Walton Beach.

Historic Pensacola Village, 205 East Zaragoza Street, Pensacola.

Heritage Museum, 115 Westview Avenue, Valparaiso.

Books to Read

The Buck Burial Mound, by Yulee W. Lazarus (Fort Walton Beach, Fla.: Temple Mound Museum, 1979).

Archaeology of Precolumbian Florida, by Jerald T. Milanich (Gainesville: University Press of Florida, 1994).

Northwest Florida Expeditions of Clarence Bloomfield Moore, edited by Davis S. Brose and Nancy Marie White (Tuscaloosa: University of Alabama Press, 1999).

2. European Explorers

In a small Spanish village, Álvar Núñez Cabeza de Vaca grew up hearing stories of exotic lands rich with gold and silver and of expeditions launched to bring these treasures home. He was fascinated by his grandfather's tales of conquering the Canary Islands, and he longed to set sail for distant lands and adventures. He would follow that dream, and he became the first known European to set foot on the Emerald Coast. His journal would be the first published words about this shore and the interior of the New World.[1]

The story begins in June 1527, at San Lucar de Barrameda, where Núñez helped to ready a fleet of five ships for a voyage of six hundred men with orders to conquer Florida.[2] A seasoned soldier at age thirty-seven, Núñez was appointed treasurer and second-in-command of the fleet. His commanding officer was Pánfilo de Narváez, a red-bearded, one-eyed explorer who had sailed on one of the seventeen ships of Columbus's second voyage in 1493.[3] After leading forays into Mexico and Cuba, where he was a top-ranking official, Narváez earned a reputation for cruelty and incompetence.[4] If Núñez could have known what awaited him because of Narváez's decisions, he would have been reluctant to go on the mission.

Núñez watched the crew load flour, cheese, sardines, and wine. They brought olive branches aboard to burn under big copper kettles used for cooking. When the ships were loaded, their hulls settling lower in the water, the sails were raised, and one by one they cruised out of the harbor. When Núñez would again see his homeland, he would be a changed man.

In the West Indies, nearly a fourth of the crew, 140 men, deserted. Then the expedition was battered by a hurricane, which swept away two ships, killing sixty of the crew and twenty horses.[5]

It was spring, April 12, nearly a year after leaving Spain, when Núñez sighted what he knew as the Land of Flowers, near Tampa Bay.[6] The Spaniards knew little about the continent whose edge they were seeing, not even its size,

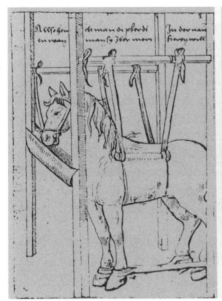

7. Horses were transported aboard ship in slings so their legs would not break in stormy seas. From *Das Trachtenbuch des Christoph Weiditz (von seinen resisen nach Spanien, 1529, und den Niederlanden, 1531–32).*

which they thought was little more than the width of Mexico. No Europeans had yet crossed America's interior.[7]

Commander Narváez decided to leave the boats and explore the land. It was a decision that would cost most of the explorers their lives.[8] Foot soldiers wore pointed metal helmets and armor formed of thousands of tiny interlinked metal rings and carried crossbows. Cavalrymen wore sheaths of leather and linen with a layer of metal. Each man carried a ration of two pounds of biscuit and a half-pound of bacon.

After trudging inland and invading native villages, the Spaniards tried to find their way back to the ships, but they would never find them. Malaria and dysentery swept through their ranks. Others died of hunger and thirst. The men agreed their only hope was to build barges and try to sail to safety. On August 4, 1528, they gathered crossbows, stirrups, and spurs to melt down and forge into axes, saws, nails, and hammers. They whacked palmettos with their swords, twisted the fronds, and shredded them into pieces of fiber to use as caulk. They wove other strips into rope. They slashed pines to bleed resin to make into pitch. They tied together shirts to make sails.[9]

Every third day, they slaughtered a horse for food. Manes and tails were braided into rope. Skin from the animal's legs was dried in the sun, rubbed with fat, and tanned into leather pouches to hold water. They stopped work several times to raid Native American villages for food and were in turn ambushed by natives.[10]

After seven weeks, the last horse was slaughtered. By then, the Spaniards

8. Caravels such as these sailed along the Emerald Coast from Europe to find good harbors. Engraving by Theodore de Bry in Girolamo Benzoni, *Americae pars quarta . . . historia . . . Occidental India* (Part IV of *Historia Americae sive Novi Orbis*), 1594.

9. The Florida peninsula dominates a sixteenth-century map drawn before the interior of the New World was explored. Drawing by Jacques Le Moyne, engraved by Theodore de Bry. Courtesy of the Birmingham Public Library.

had put together five boats, each barge "twenty-two elbow lengths" long. Loading them with the little bit of food they could scrounge, nearly fifty men jammed shoulder to shoulder on each vessel, weighing down the barges so they were barely able to float.[11]

The caravan managed to reach the sea by waterways. Wearily, the men balanced the boats in Gulf waves, steering with juniper oars and drifting up the coast. On October 27, their barges entered a bay that some historians identify as the Choctawhatchee while others contend it was Pensacola or St. Andrews. Native Americans beckoned them to thatched houses along the shore. Núñez and his fellow explorers gratefully gulped water from clay jars that stood in front of each house and devoured fish smoked on racks made of branches. Narváez in turn gave corn to the tribe and trinkets to the chief, who wore a gorgeous animal skin robe. While the men slept that night, the officers in the chief's house and the sick soldiers lying on the beach, the Native Americans attacked. The two sides fought throughout the night. Finally, several soldiers circled around the village and attacked from the rear, driving the natives away. By dawn, every Spaniard had been wounded, Núñez in the face.[12]

Núñez and the few other Spaniards who lived through the night trudged westward—for seven more years—until reaching a Spanish settlement in Mexico. By then, of the four hundred who had come to Florida, all but Núñez and three others had died. Núñez's journal was published for the king of Spain, in order to explain what went wrong with the expedition.[13] An early edition of the book in the Library of Congress likely was owned by Thomas Jefferson.[14]

In their explorations, the Spanish cut a trail of death through northwest Florida, leaving natives slain by swords and crossbows. Many more natives were exposed to European diseases their bodies had no resistance to fight. Later European explorers who marched through Florida followed Núñez's

10. The native Florida tribe called Timucuans, here depicted curing meat and fish, likely resembled early people on the Emerald Coast. Le Moyne's depiction of the natives includes long fingernails. Drawing by Jacques Le Moyne, engraved by Theodore de Bry. Courtesy of the Birmingham Public Library.

La relacion que dio Aluar nu-
ñez cabeça de vaca de lo acaefcido enlas Jndias
enla armada donde yua por gouernador y²
philo de narbaez desde el año de veynt.
y siete hasta el año ō treynta y seys
que boluio a Seuilla con tres
de su compañia.:.

11. The title page of Núñez's journal, the first account of the interior of the New World. He described a harrowing journey across the Emerald Coast that killed all but four explorers.

lead; some even marched the same path. In their wake, they left thousands more natives dead or infected with diseases that spread throughout the region. Many villages were wiped out by epidemics and famine while others were on the verge of collapse. The civilization of prehistoric peoples along the Emerald Coast vanished.[15]

It would be decades before Europeans established successful settlements here. At least eleven Spanish expeditions sailed along St. Andrews Bay, including one led by Amerigo Vespucci possibly as early as 1498. Others followed, but they did not attempt to establish a colony because they thought the pass into the bay was just a river, not realizing it offered a harbor.[16] Hernando de Soto passed St. Andrews Bay but turned north before reaching the heart of the Emerald Coast.[17] However, in 1540 he sent a captain, Diego Maldonado, west to find a harbor for Spanish ships. Maldonado scouted Choctawhatchee Bay, but he chose what would later be called Pensacola Bay instead. If he had picked Choctawhatchee Bay, the story of the Emerald Coast might have been much different.

Maldonado was struck by the beauty of the bay he called Ochuse, later named Pensacola, which had a wide channel and was protected by land on all sides. After he reported his find to de Soto, the rest of the expedition was to meet him at the bay. However, they never arrived, and a settlement did not materialize. The survivors of de Soto's party called Florida, which was marred by bogs, heat, and poisonous plants, "the worst country that is warmed by the sun."[18]

In 1559, Spain, fearing that the French would control the Gulf Coast, decided to establish a settlement at the bay Maldonado had discovered. Tristán de Luna set sail for Ochuse Bay with one thousand settlers and five hundred soldiers on thirteen ships loaded with food and tools. They arrived on August 14. If the settlement had been successful, Pensacola would have been the first colony in the New World, predating St. Augustine.

However, the Spaniards faced an immediate lack of food and supplies because storms at sea had caused the voyage to take longer than expected. The shortage of food became even more critical when, four days after the expedition arrived at the bay, a hurricane struck, killing many of the men, destroying ships, and wiping out supplies.[19] In 1992, underwater archaeologists in the bay discovered a sunken ship that is believed to have been in Luna's expedition.[20]

The mission was a disaster. Some of the men fled inland. Luna became ill and was racked by indecision.[21] The colony failed, and the area remained unsettled by Europeans for more than 125 years.[22] Spaniards subsequently scouted the area a number of times, and one explorer, Juan Jordán de Reina, called the bay "the best I have ever seen in my life." He named the bay Panzacola, as it was called by Native Americans who lived there.[23] But the Spanish took little action until 1698, when Spain again feared France or England would occupy the bay and control the northern Gulf Coast of the New World.

That year, Spanish soldiers built a fort named Santa Mariá de Galve and tried to establish a colony. By 1712, though the population of Pensacola was only 212, the settlement had a firm foothold, and the Spanish influence remains evident today in street names and architecture.[24]

The Destin area remained unsettled by Europeans during this time. Spanish, French, and English ships sailed offshore en route to and from Mexico but did not stop and build settlements here. The captains' logs of those ships are written records of the area in the seventeenth century. The logs mention natives but do not describe them.

Milan Tapia, a Spaniard, sailed along the Emerald Coast on an expedition chronicled in *Spanish Approach to Pensacola 1689–1693*:

> After sunrise on June 28 I set sail, shifting my course seaward to catch a breeze. Later, while sailing toward land with the bowlines hauled, I . . . discovered a small opening with its entrance northwest; east of this mouth is a large sand dune; north of the latter projects another piece of land covered by a growth of tall pines; a tiny, level point of white sand lies west of this opening. When one is on a northeast and southwest line with these sand dunes, the western tip of land shuts off the entrance. . . . A river called the Chicasses [Choctawhatchee] disembogues on the northeast side, and the sound extending to Pensacola bay begins at this opening.[25]

A few years later, near the turn of the century, Pierre le Moyne d'Iberville, founder of Louisiana, sighted the Emerald Coast with his brother Bienville as they sailed toward the Mississippi Delta to establish a French settlement.

> January 24, 1699. . . . At first sight of these lands one sees sand dunes, which look very white. To the north of me a medium-sized river is visible. . . . The seashore appears to be covered with rather tall trees, behind which there are prairies. The fire we saw last night is north of me, fully 10 leagues inland. . . . I had a cannon shot fired to attract the Indians to the seashore, so that I can see them tomorrow if I do not have a fair wind to sail west.[26]

During the 1700s, Spain, France, and England continued jockeying to establish trade routes in the Gulf and colonies on shore to protect their ships as they hauled riches back to Europe. The French had started a colony to the east on the St. Johns River, the Spanish settled at Pensacola, and the British plotted to take the whole region.

France captured the de Galve fort at Pensacola in 1719 but later returned it to Spain. Attacked frequently by Creeks, the fort was relocated to Santa Rosa Island. After a hurricane destroyed it in 1752, it was moved back to the mainland and named Panzacola. The village consisted of wooden huts protected by a stockade. Control shifted back and forth between Great Britain and Spain.[27]

In 1763, Spain gave up the settlement of about forty huts to Great Britain.[28] England split the region into East and West Florida, divided by the Apalachicola River, with Pensacola being the capital of West Florida.

The British surveyor Elias Durnford planned a town by plotting 80-by-160-foot lots with gardens on a nearby stream and mapping streets lined by military and public buildings.[29] The design was implemented and can be seen at the Seville Square Historic District.

Settlement was slow, however, because the town was isolated from other colonies and travel was difficult. By 1771, Pensacola had grown to about 180 houses, but it was difficult to grow crops in the sandy soil and life was harsh. Governor George Johnstone frequently clashed with the military over policies and finally was replaced. The new governor, John Eliot, was expected to restore order to a government accused of fund mismanagement, but he hanged himself.[30]

However, William Bartram, an English botanist, was impressed by Pensacola when he arrived there from Mobile in 1776: "This city commands some natural advantages, superior to any other port in this province. . . . It is delightfully situated upon gentle rising ascents environing a spacious harbor, safe and capacious enough to shelter all the navies of Europe." He estimated that several hundred people lived there and observed that they could grow indigo, rice, and corn on the surrounding land. Bartram described the governor's palace as a large stone building with a tower that had been built by the Spanish.[31]

Control of Pensacola returned to Spain in 1781 when Bernardo de Gálvez, Spanish governor of Louisiana, led an attack by thirteen hundred soldiers aboard sixty-four ships.[32] Most of the British fled, and street names were changed to Spanish ones, such as Palafox and Zaragoza.

During the 1600s and 1700s, the northern Gulf Coast was home to pirates waiting to ambush ships sailing past loaded with treasures from Mexico and Peru. Pirates hid out at Redfish Point on St. Andrews Bay. The loot of one pirate, Billy Bowlegs, is said still to be lying on the bottom of Choctawhatchee Bay.

According to legend, as Billy Bowlegs sailed home with a schooner full of stolen gold, he was spotted off the Emerald Coast by a British warship.

He ducked through the shallows of East Pass. Before the British could send smaller boats into Choctawhatchee Bay after him, Bowlegs buried what treasure he and his men could carry ashore, then sank his vessel with most of the gold.

An annual Billy Bowlegs Festival in Fort Walton Beach celebrates the legend of this pirate. The true identity of Billy Bowlegs and the location of his loot have long intrigued historians and beckoned treasure hunters. Some accounts over the years have claimed a local man was the legendary pirate. Treasure hunters even dug up that man's grave, thinking the loot might have been buried with him. Now, a different name is etched on the tombstone that stands at the head of the man's grave in an old coastal cemetery. To further complicate the matter, there also were several Seminole chiefs named Billy Bowlegs. But some say the most logical Billy Bowlegs actually was William Augustus Bowles, a political spy as well as a pirate in the late 1700s.[33]

The political scenario of that period was complicated. British expansion from colonies in the northeastern part of the country pushed Native American tribes south into the area. Tories also fled to the region to escape from British colonists who were revolting against England.

Bowles was in the thick of it all. A native of Maryland, he wound up in Pensacola after joining the British loyalists as a thirteen-year-old in 1776. By one account, he apparently was too headstrong for the military and was discharged. He joined a tribe of Creeks and married the daughter of a chief. Forming a confederation of tribes, he became a major power broker and led warriors for the British against the Spanish.

Political rule hinged on controlling trade. Bowles, still loyal to England, tried to weaken Spain's grip on the region by breaking up its trade network. He pirated Spanish ships and raided trading posts operated by the firm of Panton, Leslie and Company, a business based in Pensacola that was sanctioned by Spain to boost commerce. Spaniards hoped the people of Florida would resist joining the United States if their own economy was thriving.[34]

William Panton's company established Pensacola as the trading center of the region. The bay provided a safe harbor for his ships. He and his partner, John Leslie, befriended the Creek chief Alexander McGillivray, whose father was a Scottish trader and whose mother was a Creek, and paid him part of their profits in return for the Native American business.[35] The powerful McGillivray had organized a confederation of forty-five thousand Native

12. Panton, Leslie and Company headquarters in Pensacola was the center of trade in the region. Courtesy of State Archives of Florida.

Americans.[36] The tribes brought furs and skins to Pensacola and traded them for guns, salt, and other British goods. Traders from neighboring territories, such as Woccocoie Clarke from Alabama, traveled to Pensacola. Clarke loaded three bundles of skins, beeswax, and other goods on his horse and took them to the port town.[37]

Panton owned fifteen schooners and hundreds of packhorses to carry goods inland. He built wharves and warehouses and maintained his headquarters in Pensacola. Fifteen clerks stocked and sold the goods, an inventory valued at fifty thousand dollars, which was a fortune in those days.[38] At one time, the Panton-Leslie enterprise owned more than three million acres of land it had acquired in payment for goods sold.[39] The massive operation had branches in London, Nassau, Havana, St. Augustine, New Orleans, and Mobile.[40] The company, which grossed two hundred thousand dollars a year in the late 1700s, was hugely successful, making it a ripe target for the pirate Bowles.[41]

The Spanish plotted an elaborate trap, catching Bowles and then locking him in prisons in New Orleans and the Philippines. But the foxy pirate eventually escaped and returned to Florida, still bent on destroying Spain's trade system, again looting its forts and ships. After being captured once more, he died at the age of forty-two in a Cuban prison.[42] Whether Bowles was in fact Billy Bowlegs may always remain a mystery, but the uncertainty of the pirate's true identity adds spice to the local lore.

Despite becoming a regional trading center due to the success of Panton, Leslie and Company, Pensacola essentially remained a military post for decades.

Places to Visit

Historic Pensacola Village, Seville Square, 205 East Zaragoza Street, Pensacola.

Books to Read

Pensacola: Spaniards to Space-Age, by Virginia Parks (Pensacola: Pensacola Historical Society, 1986).

History of the Playground Area, by Leonard Patrick Hutchinson (St. Petersburg, Fla.: Great Outdoors Publishing, 1961).

3. Sam Story and the Scots

A small band of Euchees led ponies loaded with smoked fish and dried game along a rough trail to Story's Landing at Mushy Bend on the Choctawhatchee River. The year was 1820.[1]

Their tall chief, Timpoochee Kinnard, who came to be known as Sam Story, quietly supervised as they stacked the goods onto flat-bottomed barges made of logs lashed together for the journey from east Walton County to Pensacola, where the merchandise would be sold or traded. Pensacola continued to be a regional trading center that provided supplies for outlying settlements.

They wore necklaces of polished shells and beads that swayed and clinked with their movements as they loaded the barges.[2] Some wore loose-fitting shirts of coarse fabric, cinched at the waist with sashes of geometric patterned cloth.[3] Others wore animal skins or a combination of a deer-hide vest with fabric pants.

The Euchees knew they had a long way to travel, for this was a trip they made several times a year. Eventually they passed from Choctawhatchee Bay into a narrow strip of calm water that paralleled the Gulf. The water was so clear they could see the white sandy bottom of this natural channel, now called Santa Rosa Sound, that would take them to another bay at Pensacola. The journey would take about two months.[4]

The Euchees passed scenery that had been described by Bernard Romans, an assistant surveyor, in 1775. Santa Rosa Island "being no more than a long and narrow slip . . . [of] sand-hills, . . . [here] and there some groves of pine trees scattered on it; towards the west end the beech [sic] is exceedingly white, and some of the sand-hills loom like lofty white buildings, or vessels under sail, especially when not too near; the bottom here is a white sand, with here and there a spot of coral, it shoals very gradually; within the island is a sound which is from 1 to 3 miles wide, narrowest at the east end."[5]

Fields of wheat, barley, oats, and rye spread across the landscape. But the most important grain in the fields was maize. The corn was fed to pigs and poultry and was parched for a flour to be stirred into breads and puddings or cooked as mush and hominy. This coastal soil could yield fifteen to fifty bushels an acre of the valuable maize.[6]

When Sam Story reached Pensacola he encountered settlers dressed for the warm climate, wearing clothes much different from other parts of the country. Romans had described the costumes of these people. "They are very plain," he wrote, continuing, "their dress consists of a straight waistcoat of striped cotton, and a pair of trousers of the same, and often no coat; if any, it is a short one of some light stuff; in winter a kind of surtout, made of a blanket, and a pair of Indian boots is all the addition; the women also dress light and are not very expensive; happy frugality!"[7]

Story arrived in a town of just over seven hundred residents, with sand streets and crude frame buildings. Although its harbor did not have a wharf, Pensacola was by far the largest settlement in the region.[8]

The customs of the settlers were much different than those of Story's tribe. He would have been puzzled by Mardi Gras celebrations, in which the settlers dressed up in gala outfits and elaborate masks.[9] They ate jambalaya, gumbo, fish fritters, and oyster stew. Townspeople picnicked and played games such as catch the greasy pig, sack racing, and tug-of-war. Cockfights on Saturday afternoons entertained men of the town.[10]

One popular game was called patgo. Ladies decorated chickens cut out of blocks of wood with ribbons, each representing the lass who made it. The birds were mounted on a pole, and each man shot one. When their bullets cut down a ribbon, they claimed a dance with the young woman who decorated it.[11]

Fishermen were among the vendors who hawked their goods to neighborhoods. They carried the day's catch in wooden tubs suspended on poles that two men carried on their shoulders.[12]

Merchants in Pensacola told Story that a brawny Scotsman, Neill McLendon, wanted to talk to him about settling in the "new country" where the Euchees lived. The meeting between these two men was a milestone, an event that would lead to one of the first settlements by Europeans in the middle of the Emerald Coast. The story of that settlement was preserved by John L. McKinnon, the son of a McLendon friend, who described his ancestors' early pioneer days in *History of Walton County,* published in 1911.[13]

McLendon had sailed with family and friends from Liverpool, England, to North Carolina on the *Scotia,* a ship nicknamed "The Second Mayflower."

After living in Wilmington for a while, McLendon "longed for a newer and better country,—a cattle, hog and sheep range,—a home where he could have more elbow room and breathe purer air. . . . He had read of Florida, 'the land of sunshine and flowers,' of its towering pines and spreading oaks, its green pasturage, its great bays, lakes and rivers, abounding in fish, and of the mighty gulf that lashed its shores. He longed to have a plenty of everything."[14]

The region had become more appealing to McLendon and other pioneers when the War of 1812 ended. Before that, the territory had been racked by instability as Spanish, British, and French forces fought for ownership. The British were suspected of arming Native Americans to keep Federalists from claiming the area for the United States.[15]

General Andrew Jackson, who became a national hero for his victories in the War of 1812 and the First Seminole War of 1818, played a pivotal role in the politics of Pensacola. He drove the British out of the coastal town twice in the early 1800s. Pensacola was a British port during the War of 1812 until Jackson captured it in 1814. A few years later, he returned to fight Seminoles who were attacking Florida settlements near the U.S. border. Jackson wanted to make West Florida a territory of the United States, and largely due to his determination, Spain relinquished control of the region.[16]

In a formal ceremony to mark the transfer of power, Jackson and Spanish governor Jose Callava watched as the Spanish flag was lowered and the U.S. flag was raised, while a band played the "Star-Spangled Banner" followed by a twenty-one-gun salute.[17]

Cavalier yet hot-tempered, Jackson had several conflicts with the former Spanish governor of Pensacola and at one point slammed Callava in jail. During Jackson's brief term of three months, he made the port town part of America. Jackson organized the territory into two counties and established courts and civil regulations. A mayor and city council began to govern. When the process was completed, Jackson returned to Tennessee.[18]

As part of the United States, the region began to appeal to colonists such as the Scottish McLendon whom Sam Story met in Pensacola. Before coming to America, the Scottish clan might have seen notices of land grants published in the *London Gazette* or the *Scots Magazine*.[19] For the trip south, they packed flour, guns, knives, clothes, and blankets into several wagons. McLendon led the caravan of covered wagons pulled by horses out of Wilmington and on through South Carolina, Georgia, and Alabama.[20]

McLendon likely followed advice similar to that given by the naturalist Romans. Pioneers traveling to the wilderness, he said, should carry powder and shot, as well as utensils for dressing game. They should pack at least a year's supply of flour, maize, pork, and beef. Allow an hour before dark to build a fire, necessary even in summer to "rarify the air," he said. To keep from catching a cold, they should sleep on a bearskin instead of on the damp ground, and point their feet toward the fire. Be careful of the material used to tie boats to shore trees, Romans cautioned, because beavers chew through some kinds of rope, setting boats adrift during the night. When making spits for roasting meat, avoid plants found in low ground because some give off a bitter taste.[21]

By following such tips, the Scots survived the months-long journey from North Carolina. In Pensacola, they heard about Sam Story's wild but beautiful land. When the Euchee chief arrived at the trading post, he and McLendon talked, and Story agreed to let the Scots settle near his village.[22] It was the beginning of a friendly relationship that would come to be unusual for the time. Over the next two decades, white settlers moving into northwest Florida and Creeks who had come south from Alabama and Georgia, fleeing removal by the U.S. government, viewed each other skeptically. Tensions between the two groups would later flare into savage acts.

Story, however, decided to befriend the Scots. He told the Scotsman to follow an inland trail. McLendon prepared to journey again, making sure he had enough bullets for his long Scottish-made Buchanan rifle. McKinnon described the journey that followed: "With their guns and packs on their backs, they followed this dimly beaten path, wading, swimming, or pontooning the creeks and rivers that fell across their way."[23]

At Story's village, the Euchees welcomed the Scots with a strong black drink, venison, and cornbread. A large ceremonial tent formed the heart of the settlement. Trails branched out in different directions, one leading to a cornfield, another to a tannery. Ponies drank from a trough carved out of a large boulder of "sand rock" from Rock Hill. Nearby, the soil was packed into a circle of hard ground, having been pounded year after year by the Euchees dancing their "green corn" celebration of harvest.[24]

There have been several spellings of "Euchee." The botanist Bartram visited an "Uche" Indian village in 1775 while trekking through the Southeast before the country became a nation, keeping a journal describing the plants and people he came across in the unsettled frontier. The village Bartram described might have been similar to Sam Story's settlement. On a swift river three hundred yards wide—the "Chata Uche," near present-day Phenix City, Alabama—Uches paddled over in big canoes and helped Bartram cross to their village on an elevated plain:

> It is the largest, most compact and best situated Indian town I ever saw; the habitations are large and neatly built; the walls of the houses are constructed of a wooden frame, then lathed and plaistered [sic] inside and out with a reddish well tempered clay or morter [sic], which gives them the appearance of red brick walls, and these houses are neatly covered or roofed with Cypress bark or shingles of that tree. The town appeared to be populous and thriving, full of youth and young children: I suppose the number of inhabitants, men, women and children, might amount to one thousand or fifteen hundred, as it is said they are able to muster five hundred gun-men or warriors. Their own national language is altogether or radically different from the Creek or Muscogulge tongue, and is called the Savanna or Savanuca tongue; I was told by the traders it was the same or a dialect of the Shawanese. They are in confederacy with the Creeks, but do not mix with them, and on account of their numbers and strength, are of importance enough to excite and draw upon them the jealousy of the whole Muscogulge confederacy, and are usually at variance, yet are wise enough to unite against a common enemy, to support the interest and glory of the general Creek confederacy.
>
> After a little refreshment at this beautiful town, we repacked and set off again.[25]

With Sam Story and a sundial as their guides, the Scots explored the land, skirting swamps, following creeks, passing lakes and springs, and admiring the landscape where nature was unspoiled.[26]

McLendon and his friends cleared plots to plant corn and cut small trees to build bungalows of round logs. They ground corn into flour for bread, roasted deer and rabbits, and drank rum, which provided an added benefit of killing intestinal bacteria.[27]

The settlers hunted bear and squirrels to keep the animals from eating the corn growing in their fields. The Scots debated whether to confine their cattle and hogs with fences or let them roam freely. If fenced, the animals would have to be fed. If turned loose, the cattle and hogs could graze but could be attacked by wild animals, so they fenced them. The settlers slaughtered pigs in the fall and tanned cowhide, which replaced deerskin.

They heard the occasional twang of bowstrings, the ring of an ax, gunshots of a hunter, and chants of Euchee ceremonies. But the sounds of nature dominated: "At night the happy mocker, perched up on the highest limb, leads the chorus for the night, the whip-poor-will in the distance chimes in with its plaintive lays, while the horned owl from the swamp joins in with his deep bass voice, joining in the chorus with the other birds. . . . The dawn is ushered in by the strutting gobbler, with his commanding voice, answered by the deep baritone voice of the long-legged and long-necked sand-hill-crane, that ever keeps watch around the ponds and lakes."[28]

Sam Story, remembered as the area's first conservationist, urged the pioneers to preserve grassy meadows, forests, fish, and animals. He urged them to only shoot deer and other game in certain seasons to avoid depleting them and to only kill animals for food or skins. Always watch campfires, he warned, to keep them from searing berries and apple trees and burning grasses that would be replaced by "worthless" scrub oak.[29] However, Story likely adapted the practice of other Native Americans in the South of intentionally burning longleaf pine forests if lightning-ignited fires did not occur every three to five years. Fire was important to the survival of longleaf pines because it enabled pine seedlings to take hold without the shade of hardwoods that would become dominant. Longleaf pines are fire resistant at nearly every stage of growth.[30]

The Euchees likely fished in ways similar to other Native Americans of the Southeast, using fishhooks of deer and turkey bones or of the wishbones of birds. The hooks were attached to a shank, baited, and then put on a trotline that was strung across a stream. Every few hours, the Euchees checked the line and removed fish caught, then put fresh bait on the hooks.

They also made hoop nets that scooped up the fish. Animal hide soaked in fresh blood was also dipped into the water to attract catfish, then closed with a string.

Tribe members shot arrows with string attached to pierce a fish and pull it ashore. They speared fish from canoes with pointed green canes or tips made from horseshoe crab and stingrays. In shallow water, the Euchees poisoned fish by scattering buckeye nuts and devil's shoestring root. When the fish floated to the surface, the fishermen scooped them up.[31]

Back in North Carolina, John L. McKinnon eagerly read an eight-page letter from his close friend McLendon describing this frontier. McKinnon then passed the pages around to family and neighbors and decided to head for Florida himself. He hitched his stallion, "Jack," to a two-wheel cart and with his black worker, George, set out for Florida to join the settlement. Standing six feet, six inches tall and weighing only 185 pounds, McKinnon was all muscle. A story was told of McKinnon being so strong that he had once twisted the legs off a steer with his bare hands.[32]

By the end of the decade, some twelve hundred people had settled in Walton County, which was much larger then than today, according to the first census of the area taken in 1830.[33] There was "not quite a half man to the square mile," wrote McKinnon.

Meanwhile, the Scots and other settlers herded cattle, sheep, and hogs and planted cotton in their fields. The older women spent evenings pulling seed from cotton picked by settlers, then spinning and weaving the fibers into fabric. For vacations, they gathered at a rustic lodge at Ponce de Leon Spring a few miles to the north.[34]

Pioneers often faced danger. The Scots discovered that the untamed country could turn vicious, and deadly, with yellow fever, a snakebite, or storm. Wolves often slaughtered the settlers' sheep. Bears roamed freely in the woods. Willie Howell, about six or eight years old, was following his mother on a trail near Eucheeanna when a panther leaped from the bushes onto his back. The mother grabbed a tree limb and beat the animal until it died.[35]

There were also times of celebration. The Euchees and the Scots watched

Pioneer Families of Walton County		
McLendon	Campbell	Folk
McKinnon	Hunter	Jones
McCarter	Henderson	McLean
McDonald	McKenzie	Purcil
McSween	Anderson	Albin
McCaskill	McGilberrie	Ramsey
McQuaig	Mallet	Robinson
McCallum	Rector	McLean

John L. McKinnon, The History of Walton County, 41.

with curiosity as Chief Story's handsome oldest son, Jim Crow, fell in love with a pretty servant girl of McKinnon's wife. The girl, Harriet, at first turned him away, to the relief of her masters, who worried about a union of the two cultures. But Jim Crow eventually won her over, and a grand marriage ceremony was planned.

The wedding took place on a Sunday. Friends and family escorted the bride and groom, dressed in their finery, to the chief's grand tent. The happy couple met in front of the tent, which was open to the breeze with its sides rolled up, and enjoying the strains of merry music, they joined hands and marched with their attendants around the tent several times. Then they entered the tent, and Chief Story conducted the ceremony in the Euchee language. To end the ceremony, the couple jumped over a broom and became man and wife.[36]

The serene atmosphere would not last long. As Sam Story sadly watched, the increasing number of travelers and settlers ruined much of the land and its wildlife. More settlers cleared land for fields by burning cut trees and bushes. Many of the newcomers shot game for sport and clear-cut trees recklessly with their saws.[37]

The area joined the rest of the South in struggling with the issue of whether to use natural resources freely or to enact conservation measures to protect wildlife. The region's natural wealth was being depleted; the land Story loved was in peril. He saw some animal species, such as the Florida wolf, decline radically. Some animals were overhunted, while others disappeared because their habitats were destroyed.

In the colonial period of the 1800s, some parts of the South passed laws to conserve trees or animals, but these laws were largely ignored. The Euchee chief and Scottish settlers held a meeting in the early 1830s to discuss what they could do to halt the growing problem. Story said he was puzzled about why the newcomers had been setting fires to expansive plots, and he was told that they were burning rattlesnakes. They paid him little mind when he explained that the rattlers would just crawl into their holes. McLendon said hunters who had set fire to canebrakes had told him they simply wanted to hear the cane pop. The newcomers had laughed when McLendon told them they were destroying grasses that fed cattle; they believed that there was plenty.[38]

Story suggested that the Euchees and Scots move east. But McKinnon thought they should try to educate the newcomers about protecting resources. He said the same problems would be found in other places. In 1832, the chief went east and south along the Atlantic Coast with several sons and tribesmen to scout out the territory. After searching for six months, he came back and reported that he saw areas that were better in some ways and lacking in others. Still, he began getting his tribe ready to move.[39]

However, Story was old, and the scouting trip had exhausted him. Soon after returning, he sent for McKinnon; his good friend Neill McLendon was already at the chief's tent. Story told them the Great Spirit was calling him. Family and friends gathered around him. Dying—of despair, some say—Story told his son Jim Crow to lead the tribe with honor. Story asked to be buried in a coffin with his unstrung bow, an arrow, and a tomahawk by his side. His grave would be dug in the shade of great trees near Story's Landing in the highlands of Walton County.[40]

The grave remains there today, near the community of Redbay. Occasionally visited by those who have heard the tale of Sam Story and the Scots, the burial site is on private property. After his death, the Euchees packed their belongings, and with Jim Crow as their chief they went east; McKinnon believes they traveled to the Everglades, where they merged with the Seminoles. Jim Crow's wife, Harriet, remained behind in Walton County with their children, who grew up and had youngsters of their own. McLendon built a boat, sailed to Texas with his family, and settled near Waco.[41]

The Scots who remained in Walton County faced a period of terror in the 1830s.[42] Creeks who felt white settlers were driving them from their land began attacking pioneers. In July 1834, just thirty-five miles north of the Walton County settlement of Alaqua, Creeks killed an eighteen-year-old white man who might have confronted them over stealing livestock. White settlers tracked down the natives, killed one, and wounded two. Such incidents fed the fears of white settlers who were apprehensive that the Creeks might join with the Seminoles then fighting the U.S. government in the Second Seminole War.[43]

Most Creeks in Bay County, where Panama City is today, did not participate in raids on white settlers. However, Native Americans killed a woman and two of her children because they thought she tried to poison them with eggs that had pepper on them. And bands of Seminoles massacred settlers. One of the raiders was the infamous Indian Joe, who finally was killed during a knife fight with a trader.[44]

In 1837, small bands of Creeks followed the Choctawhatchee River, stealing goods along the way. An entire family, the Albersons, was murdered on February 28 at the Florida-Alabama border.[45] It was the beginning of a year of brutal killings in Walton County that spread panic through the area.

In the Panhandle, Walton County was hit hardest by the violence. The U.S. Superior Court decided to suspend its session in the county, and Florida governor Richard Call issued rations to the needy because the economy was so disrupted. The U.S. Indian agent Archibald Smith heard that four hundred Creeks were hiding in wild forests between Pensacola and the Apalachicola River. He warned settlers that Creeks were taking refuge north of Choctawhatchee Bay.[46]

Then, in the area where Milton is today, an incident occurred that would lead to tremendous tragedy in Walton County. On April 15, white men tied a rope around a Creek man's neck and pulled him under lumber in the river until he drowned. The Creeks retaliated. John McKinnon heard the story as a boy while sitting around a campfire tending cattle, and he wrote it down later in life. Sill Caswell told him a band of Creeks had killed the entire Joseph family, except for a daughter who the warriors thought was dead but who survived. Caswell and a friend survived another attack by Creeks that left several on each side killed.[47]

The military tried to convince the Creeks to leave and join Native Americans from other areas migrating to the West. Some seventy decided to go, and they were taken to Mobile Point.[48]

However, the killing did not stop. In May 1837, Native Americans killed some dozen white settlers in Walton County. Terror spread through the county, and a militia was formed. A group of drunken white settlers subsequently killed a native named Jim who had been a guide and interpreter.

The *Pensacola Gazette* criticized the white settlers in a blistering editorial: "It is high time that these unprincipled wretches should be made to pay with their lives, the penalty of thus violating the laws of the land, and shedding human blood." The paper continued: "The Indian, when friendly and peaceable, is as much entitled to the protection of our laws, as the best man in the community."[49] But the call for obeying the law had little effect. Soon after, militiamen from Jackson County, northwest of Walton County on the Alabama and Georgia borders, came upon a group of Native Americans at Alaqua Creek and killed at least nine women and children.[50]

Other skirmishes followed as the militia tracked down Creeks. The raids by militia over the summer persuaded most of the Native Americans to surrender. Most were removed except for small bands that hid in isolated areas. They merged into white or black communities and tried to conceal themselves by giving up their culture. The historian Brian R. Rucker described the prices paid by both cultures: "For the white frontiersmen it was a tragic episode—families brutally murdered, property destroyed and stolen, and settlements terrorized with fear." But "for the Native Americans it was a more lasting tragedy—many were killed, hundreds were deported to the West, and the remaining natives were condemned to poverty and the loss of their heritage and culture."[51]

Oddly enough, the Creek wars opened the region to more settlements. Soldiers cut trails across the state for military wagons and built forts to defend their positions, thus providing both transportation and protection for new waves of settlers.

Pensacola, as the capital of the territory, hosted the first Florida Legislative Council, which was attended by thirteen members in 1822. A yellow fever epidemic struck, and delegates moved to the home of a local resident. Some 237 people died during the epidemic, including the council's president, James Bronaugh, Andrew Jackson's doctor. It was the only time the council met in Pensacola.[52] Trails that soldiers had cut were so crude that members from St. Augustine traveled by boat to the Pensacola meeting. The trip took fifty-nine days, and after Pensacola members had an equally difficult time reaching St. Augustine for the next meeting, the capital was moved to Tallahassee, which was halfway in between.[53]

Soon after losing the capital, Pensacola gained a navy yard in 1825: "Pensacola and the U.S. Navy had begun a long and profitable relationship," noted the historian Virginia Parks. The port city was chosen for the navy yard because it had a deep harbor and an abundance of live oaks, but construction of the navy yard was slow because of a shortage of materials and skilled labor. Commodore Lewis Warrington was the first commandant. He set aside lots on government property near the yard for civilian workers to lease and build homes.[54] When completed, the yard established Pensacola as an important naval base, which it continues to be today.

The Naval Live Oaks Reservation was established near present-day Gulf Breeze to protect trees slated for use in shipbuilding. These beautiful live oaks with their graceful limbs were an important resource, vital to national security. The rot-resistant wood, so strong that cannonballs often bounced off the hulls, was perfect for building sturdy ships that would protect the country's coasts from invaders.

The historian Albert James Pickett visited the keeper of the live-oak reservation on Santa Rosa Sound in 1858 and described what he saw there: "The yard and the gardens abound with orange trees and fine fruit trees of all varieties. . . . Splendid live-oaks, with their verdant leaves, encircle the premises on three sides, contributing to render the whole place an earthly Paradise." The keeper was paid fifteen hundred dollars a year by the federal government and had two servants.[55]

Gradually, crude roads were built throughout the Emerald Coast, including one that linked Pensacola and Tallahassee. Settlers moved to the St. Andrews Bay area, where Choctaw and Apalachee tribes from Chipley and Marianna had camped in winters so they could fish and collect oysters.[56]

The retired governor of Georgia John Clark was one of the first white settlers. He built a large log home in 1827 at what became the town of St. Andrews.[57] Others included men like William T. Loftin, who had scouted the area for Andrew Jackson, and Peter Gautier, a Methodist minister who was a missionary to Native Americans.[58] A Pensacola attorney who traveled through the Emerald Coast in 1827 reported that forty families were living in the St. Andrews Bay area. Inland pioneers who came to the shore to vacation joined fishermen who made their living from the water, selling oysters for one dollar per thousand. The visitors arrived by wagon in small groups, camping in tents along the way. At the bay, wooden steps led to the water, and bathhouses were built for those taking "sea baths," short dips of a couple of minutes, taken medicinally, followed by a nap.

A Kentucky pioneer named Payton Short wrote on December 17, 1809, from Pensacola, "I found beef the only cheap article in this place. Every thing sold uncommonly high. Chickens at one dollar each. Bacon from 25 to 50 cents per lb. Flour 20$ per barrel. Sweet potatoes 2$ per bushel. Pumpkins from 37 1/2 to 50 cents each. Turnips 6 1/4 cents each. Milk one dollar per quart. Eggs one dollar per dozen and every other article in proportion."

Payton Short, *Annual Report of the Historical and Philosophical Society of Ohio*, December 17, 1809.

The Old Town at St. Andrews Bay was a resort in the 1820s. When a post office opened in 1845, the town had a summer population of twelve hundred.[59]

At about the same time, a young Connecticut seaman named Leonard Destin set sail for the south with his father and brother. He would leave his own unique mark on the Emerald Coast.

Places to Visit

Historic Pensacola Village, with museums, furnished houses of the 1800s, and a colonial archaeology trail, 205 East Zaragoza Street, Pensacola.

Fort Pickens, where Geronimo, chief of the Chiricahua Apaches, was imprisoned, at Gulf Islands National Seashore, on Fort Pickens Road at Pensacola Beach on the western end of Santa Rosa Island.

Historical Museum, 115 Westview Avenue, Valparaiso.

Books to Read

History of Walton County, by John L. McKinnon (1911; reprint, Gainesville, Fla: Palmetto Books, 1968; text also available on the Internet).

William Bartram: Travels and Other Writings, by William Bartram, with notes by Thomas P. Slaughter (1791; reprint, New York: Library of America, 1996).

4. Leonard Destin's Fishing Legacy

Leonard Destin, his muscles hard and hands rough from months at sea, arrived at a desolate sand spit that reached like a crab claw between the Gulf of Mexico and Choctawhatchee Bay.

The young man must have longed to share this new frontier with his father, George, and brother, William, who had both been lost at sea. The three had sailed the length of the continent from New London, Connecticut, where Leonard had been born on August 31, 1813, to George and Fanny Rogers Destin.[1]

By one account, during the voyage midway down the Atlantic side of the Florida peninsula at Cape Canaveral, a tropical gale whipped their boat with high winds and surf. Soaked with spray from crashing giant swells, they struggled to hold the helm steady. But George and William perished.[2]

Destin pushed on, toughened by tragedy, past stretches of mangroves and marshes. He rounded the tip of the peninsula into calmer Gulf waters that washed the shore curving west and eventually came to Choctawhatchee Bay, where years later a village would be named for him.

The Gulf water was so clear that Destin could see schools of pompano darting into the wash near shore to feed on sand fleas. He noticed that a wide sandy shelf extending under the Gulf provided shallow water for net fishing.

Hills of white sand lined the coast, nearly hiding green stands of pines and live oaks where bobcats prowled. The dunes were marked by tracks of black bears that lumbered along the beach at night searching for loggerhead turtle eggs, which were laid by the hundred just beyond the high tide surf.[3] Grasses grew tall in meadows that framed the shore.

Destin explored the coastal waters, liking what he saw. He sailed through a slit of water, East Pass, into Choctawhatchee Bay. On the inland side of the sandy claw, the bay offered shelter from the sea with a quick route to Gulf fishing.

Across the bay, Destin found scattered homesteads. He hired several men to be his fishing crew. They built shanties, similar to Old West bunkhouses, on the shore.[4] This rugged, pioneer fishing camp was the beginning of a tradition that continues today, luring anglers by the thousands.

Destin's crew arrived each spring to bunk at the camp until fishing season ended in November. They tied heavy cotton twine into a huge seine net shaped like a pocket. They dipped the net in drums of boiling tar for waterproofing, then salted and soaked it in water for several days. Floats carved from auburn-colored juniper were tied to the top of the pocket, and lead weights were anchored onto the bottom.

At dawn, the fishermen would crawl into a small wooden yawl about fourteen feet long. Pulling oars that were six feet longer than the boat, they swept the vessel through Gulf water.[5]

Captain "Len" stood at the prow or on the shore, scanning the water for darting shadows. In the spring, the fishermen rowed east to intercept fish migrating west. They took the opposite tack in the fall when fish migrated east.[6]

Destin had good eyes for spotting a school of fish. Two men manning the oars swung the boat around in front of the school, while a third crewman tried to net the fish before they disappeared. When the net encircled fish, the men steered the boat into water waist deep. A couple of crewmen slid over the side and pulled in the net. The men with the strongest legs held the bottom of the seine with their feet, trapping fish in its pocket.

They pulled the net onto the beach and loaded mullet, mackerel, pompano, sheepshead, and red snapper into a well in the boat. When the compartment was full, they returned to the dock, where some fish were packed in ice, which was insulated by sawdust. Other fish were salted and pickled to be sold as snapper bait, or to eat.[7] The rest of the catch was loaded aboard Destin's schooner the *Hempstead* and sailed to market in Pensacola, where it would ship out for northern markets.

In addition to the booming seafood industry, Pensacola's economy was getting a boost from the military, which decided to build a fort to protect the navy yard. The job of constructing the fort was given to West Point graduate William H. Chase of the Army Corps of Engineers, who would certainly leave his mark on the port city. Chase encouraged local businessmen to build kilns and make bricks from the area's clay for construction of the fort. A new industry was born. Then Chase convinced the army to build two more forts, which further boosted the building and supply trades over the next ten years.[8] At one company, Bacon and Abercrombie, 102 workers produced eight million bricks in one year.[9]

Chase has been called Pensacola's "economic patriarch," credited with laying a stable base of prosperity for the city, like the sturdy bricks of his forts. He joined businessmen in working to get a railroad from Pensacola to Alabama and another to Georgia.

The military presence greatly influenced Pensacola socially as well as economically. One navy officer described the town as "the paradise of midshipmen," who loved the gaiety of the seaport and the pretty girls.[10]

Alabama wanted to annex the Pensacola area, but in 1845 the entire territory of Florida joined the Union as a slave state.[11] For a time, Pensacola's growth slowed, probably because of yellow fever epidemics that killed 260 out of its population of 1,200.[12] Almost every family lost someone to the disease. Yet Pensacola managed to survive. "No entrance to any bay on any portion of the globe, can surpass this, for utility, beauty and safety," wrote the historian Albert James Pickett.[13]

Another writer stopped in Pensacola on a boating adventure from Pennsylvania in 1876. Twenty-five-year-old Nathaniel H. Bishop had cruised down the Ohio and Mississippi rivers to the Gulf of Mexico and then followed the coast to northwest Florida. Pilots and fishermen welcomed him at the navy yard. He crossed the bay and saw, on the west end of Santa Rosa Island, Fort Pickens rising "gloomily" out of the sand.[14] It was the only structure except for a small cabin. As he entered Santa Rosa Sound from Pensacola Bay, "the morning of the 19th of February was calm and beautiful, while the songs of mockingbirds filled the air."[15]

The air was still, so Bishop rowed his twelve-foot boat instead of hoisting the sail. Partway down the forty-mile Santa Rosa Sound, Bishop camped at the base of dunes with a friend he made along the way and with some native raccoons. An old fisherman had told him the woods on the mainland were full of bobcats and panthers. The next morning, he climbed to the top of the tallest dune for a "fine view of the boundless sea," and then he pushed east.

> Before noon a sail appeared on the horizon, and we gradually approached it. Close to the shore we saw a raft of sawed timbers being towed by a yacht. The captain hailed us, and we were soon alongside his vessel. The refined features of a gentleman beamed upon us from under an old straw hat, as its owner trod,

barefoot, the deck of his craft. He had started, with the raft in tow, from his mill at the head of Choctawhatchee Bay, bound for the great lumber port of Pensacola, but being several times becalmed, was now out of provisions. We gave him and his men all we could spare from our store.

The stranded gentleman was a former Confederate general, possibly William Miller, who had commanded a Florida battalion during the war and afterward owned an area sawmill. He warned Bishop to watch for a scoundrel farther east.

Bishop continued down Santa Rosa Sound to Choctawhatchee Bay. He passed a few shanties "beguiled to this desolate region by the sentimental idea of pioneer life in a fine climate known as 'FLORIDA FEVER.'" He said settlers were starving on a fish diet and braving insects. The wind picked up. Bishop turned into East Pass and sailed into an inlet of the bay.

> Here we encountered an original character known as "Captain Len Destin." He was a fisherman, from New London, Connecticut, and had a comfortable house on the high bank of the inlet, surrounded by cultivated fields, where he had lived since 1852. Having married a native of the country, he settled down to the occupation of his fathers; and being a prince among fishermen, he was able to send good supplies of the best fish to the Pensacola markets. . . .
>
> Captain Len generously supplied our camp with fish; so making a good fire, we broiled them before it, baking bread in our Dutch oven; and finishing our sumptuous repast with some hot coffee, we turned a deaf ear to the whistling wind that blew steadily from the north-east.[16]

The woman Destin married was Martha J. McCullom from South Carolina.[17] He probably enjoyed hearing Martha's southern accent, but he was known as a man of few words himself. Their home still stands on Calhoun Avenue, on the bay, but the Destin family does not own it. The house was to be handed down to Captain Len's son George, but he refused it because his father and mother had both died there and, besides, he had a home of his own, according to Muriel R. Destin, the widow of Dewey E. "Buck" Destin Sr., Leonard's great-grandson. When Leonard lived there, huge oaks grew all the way down to the water, she said, recalling stories told to her by Leonard's grandson John. He told her Leonard had had another structure, one that stood on land where the midpoint of the Destin Bridge is now.[18] Before the current East Pass was formed, the channel had been farther east from where it is today. The federal government designated the area Moreno Point Military Reservation in 1842 to protect the live oaks that were prized for shipbuilding.

The Destins, like other settlers, were self-sufficient. The family had a shed where they salted fish and canned vegetables from their garden. They bought staples twice a year in Pensacola.[19]

A few other pioneers arrived over the years, building cabins on the sound or on bayous of the Choctawhatchee. One of them was Jesse Rogers, who drove a herd of cream-colored Charolais cattle from Louisiana to Boggy Bayou near today's town of Niceville. The prized breed of cattle was named for a region in France where it originated. A Mexican industrialist imported some after he saw them during World War I, and he later sold several to a Texas ranch.

Rogers moved his family across the bay to a tract on the sound that would become Mary Esther, where his cows grazed in meadows of coastal grasses. At sundown, Rogers built fires to keep bears from devouring his pigs.[20] Another settler was a Frenchman, Garnier, who lived on a bayou at the west end of the bay.[21] These pioneers lived miles from each other, separated by water, marsh, thick scrub, and virgin forests. They traveled by boat, for there was no bridge connecting the settlements that would become Fort Walton and Destin.

"Miasma," unhealthy air, was believed to plague the coastal lowlands that were barely above sea level. In fact, the lowlands were home to mosquitoes, bred by the millions, which carried malaria and yellow fever.

Florida's population soared from about 35,000 in 1830 to nearly 55,000 in 1840. But only 1,461 people were counted in all of Walton County in 1840, then a huge tract that included what is now Okaloosa County. By 1850, the state could claim a population of more than 87,000, with settlers heavily populating the north Florida region in general. However, in Walton County the numbers only increased by 356 people, although the low figure could partly be explained by the fact that the county shrank by giving up land to Holmes County.[22]

William T. Marler sailed across Choctawhatchee Bay from his home in Boggy Bayou to East Pass in 1879 when he was thirteen years old so he could crew for Leonard Destin.[23] Captain Len taught the youngster everything he knew, from making nets to spotting shadows cast by schools of fish. Destin died in 1884 at the age of seventy-one. He and his wife Martha are buried at the Marler Cemetery of Destin.[24]

Marler, called Captain Billy, and others like him carried on the fishing tradition in the settlement that came to be known as the World's Luckiest Fishing Village. At the age of eighty-two, Captain Billy's daughter, Willie Mae Marler Taylor, talked about that era in an interview in the small, white-frame building that had been the old post office in Destin. It is now filled with mementos and memories, and she has since passed away.

In the interview, Mrs. Taylor stated that fishing "is born in them from New England." Her ancestors had settled the area, the Marlers in Destin and the Brookses in Fort Walton Beach. Sitting on a stool in the post office, Mrs. Taylor recalled how a handful of families established this fishing village. She talked about her father handling the mail for half a century, followed by four more Marler postal workers including herself.[25]

Her father, Captain Billy, personified a way of life unique to the Gulf. In December 1955, his ninetieth year, he was profiled in *Reader's Digest* by his longtime friend William Columbia Pryor. In "The Most Unforgettable Character I've Met: Portrait of a Fast-Disappearing Breed," Pryor captured the man and his spirit.

13. Willie Mae Marler Taylor described the history of the fishing village of Destin. Her ancestors were among the first European settlers of the Emerald Coast. Photo by Jean Lufkin Bouler.

Captain Billy was the village undertaker, coffin maker, lighthouse tender, store owner, Sunday school teacher, and sometimes preacher—not to mention boatbuilder and furniture maker. His home was the center of the village. In 1899, he set up a post office in his parlor and named the village Destin in honor of the man who taught him how to fish. The first school was held in his home. Church services were held there, too.[26]

He became a legend in 1915 when he set out to rescue a crew in a boat that was going down in stormy seas. Other men cautioned that going out into the Gulf would be suicide, but Captain Billy ignored them and raced for his boat with George Destin close behind. They hopped aboard and plunged through East Pass, fighting twenty-foot waves. At times the men watching from the shore lost sight of Captain Billy's boat. Captain Billy and Destin bravely climbed from their boat into a skiff they had towed and rowed through the crashing swells to the sinking schooner. Nine crewmen had been washed overboard and were holding onto the sail, foundering in the turbulent Gulf. The skiff could only hold half of the men at a time. Captain Billy and Destin took aboard five and struggled to get back to Captain Billy's boat. They knew they couldn't leave the rest to drown, so they rowed again to the capsized boat and rescued the rest.[27]

Captain Billy was fond of telling stories about hidden treasure. Pryor said Captain Billy took him to Joe's Bayou, pointing to a spot under a cluster of oaks where a New Orleans rogue supposedly buried sixty thousand dollars in the mid-1800s. Captain Billy watched tourists who had come to hunt for treasure pitch tents and speculate about where in Choctawhatchee Bay a pirate, perhaps Billy Bowlegs, had sunk a schooner weighted with four million dollars in gold. Yet Captain Billy left the treasure hunting for others. "Why, sure, there's treasure out there!" Pryor quoted him as saying. "Where? Why, right out there!" He waved to encompass the world: "All you got to do is find it."[28]

A strong man, Captain Billy dove for turtles in Gulf shallows, once coming up with a six-hundred-pounder. On calm days, when Destin's schooner *Jack'a Don't Care* stalled dead in the water for lack of a breeze, Captain Billy pushed it forward with a stout pine pole to deliver fish to Pensacola before the catch could spoil. At age seventy, he could crumple a beer can with two fingers.[29]

But the true test of Captain Billy's mettle was the harsh, pioneer coast itself. He saw ten of his nineteen children die as infants. His wife died. Then one of his sons by his second marriage fell off his boat and drowned in the bay when the child was only two years old. His oldest son was murdered at a lighthouse he tended.[30]

However, Captain Billy's sorrows only made him more determined to help others and to leave a mark on life. "I think of all the good boats he has built," wrote Pryor, "the mail he has carried, the lights he has kept burning along the reefs, the lives he has saved from the sea, the flourishing community he has done more than any other man to build." Local historian Vivian Mettee called Captain Billy "the spirit of Destin."[31]

Over the years, other local fishermen made their living from the Gulf. They included Leonard Destin Jr., Odom T. Melvin, Homer Jones, and many others who loved the sea. John Maltezos, who at sixteen left Greece as a cabin boy to come to America, made his way to the Emerald Coast and became a boatbuilder. One craft that earned him praise was well-known fisherman John Melvin's *Primrose*, which has been preserved as a symbol of the area's fishing history.[32]

Seine boats outfitted with newly invented engines became significantly larger in the early 1900s. Some measured forty feet long and could accommodate larger nets. Meanwhile, the fishermen devised techniques for hauling in a more bountiful catch. A sounding lead with beeswax or octagon soap attached to the end was lowered and dragged on the bottom of the Gulf. If coral stuck to it, fish were likely to be found. White, red, and blue leather markers indicated the depth of the water.[33]

Lines that could be two and a half miles long were set to catch grouper and other fish. Hooks were attached every twenty feet with weights to sink the line. Buoys with colored flags floated on top of the water to mark the line.[34] Some fishermen stayed at sea for three days and hauled in five thousand to ten thousand pounds of fish.[35]

The fish were iced down and taken to E. E. Saunders or the Warren Fish Company in Pensacola to be sold. Some fish were pickled and sold by Lee Lancaster of Rocky Bayou.[36]

Fishermen also caught mullet, flounder, and sturgeon in Choctawhatchee Bay and River. Pearl and Marion Brown of Freeport fed six children by selling shrimp and oysters and running a fish camp from a houseboat. Pearl said that after Marion died, she caught flounder every night by herself, loaded them in a wheelbarrow, and sold them to a nearby store.[37]

Anglers told a tale that they knew where sturgeon could be found by feeling the bottom of submerged logs. If the log was smooth and grooved, a sturgeon had been there scratching his back. A good catch was fifteen to twenty sturgeon a week. The fish weighed an average of one hundred pounds. The sturgeon were kept fresh by driving stakes in shallow water and tying a rope from it to the fish tails.[38] Because their numbers have declined, sturgeon are now federally protected in spring when they spawn.

Anglers caught a bounty of fish. Thomas Godwin of the Freeport area remembered catching seventeen hundred pounds of speckled trout one day.[39]

Word of the good fishing waters on the Emerald Coast spread when the area became more accessible around 1930 when the road that is now U.S. Highway 98 was built. Some local residents outfitted boats to carry paying passengers to deep-sea sport fishing. One of the first such boats was the *Martha-Gene,* owned by Coleman Kelly and captained by Lee Chambless.

After World War II, as roads were paved and Destin Bridge was built, more fishermen discovered the Emerald Coast. Road crews from Tennessee bought property and spread the word about the area. Fishing boats became more sophisticated. "We used to have five-horsepower motors; now we have 500 horsepower," said Jewel Melvin. He retired from fishing and opened a seafood restaurant. "When we used to snapper fish, we had a compass and a sounding lead. Nowadays they've got radar, Lorans and all kinds of electronics."[40]

Over the next several decades, dozens of charter vessels were added to the fleet, and fishing rodeos were launched. The desolate harbor that Leonard Destin found now docks more than a hundred charter boats and lures thousands of anglers to the waters that Captain Len loved.

Places to Visit

Destin Fishing Museum, 20009 Emerald Coast Parkway, Suite B, Destin.

East Pass and Destin Harbor, at U.S. Highway 98 Bridge in Destin.

Old Destin Post Office Museum, 306 Bayshore Drive, Destin.

Books to Read

Destin History: . . . And the Roots Run Deep, by Vivian Foster Mettee and associates (Destin, Fla.: Vivian Foster Mettee and Associates, 1970).

Our Town (Fort Walton Beach, Fla.: Northwest Florida Daily News, 1992).

5. Civil War

The women of Walton County took to the streets of Eucheeanna in the spring of 1861 to encourage their men to join the Confederate army. "I would rather be a brave man's widow than a coward's wife," they chanted on the eve of the Civil War. Sixty of their men signed up with the Walton Guard, headed by Captain William McPherson, whose father was a local attorney.[1]

Music rang out at an all-night dance to send off the troops. The next day, carrying shotguns and Buchanan rifles, the new soldiers hugged their children, kissed their wives or girlfriends, and boarded the steamship *Lady of the Lake*. They cruised to the mouth of Choctawhatchee Bay with orders to guard East Pass and the "Narrows," Santa Rosa Sound.[2] On the bank of Santa Rosa Sound, where Fort Walton Beach is today, near the tallest of several mounds, the soldiers cut saplings to build a cluster of cabins they called Camp Walton.[3]

It might seem surprising that the women in Walton County would feel so fervently that their men should risk their lives for the war. Florida hardly seemed a likely location for an uproar over slavery. The sparsely settled land, with the Gulf on one side and the Atlantic on the other, seemed barely connected to the rest of the country, geographically or politically. Like the toe of a giant, the peninsula was far from the nation's heart and soul, weeks by horse or by wagon from the politics of Washington and the commerce of Boston. Yet the first shots of the war were almost fired at the back door of the Emerald Coast. A showdown in Pensacola between the state of Florida and the federal government occurred three months before the battle of Fort Sumpter started the war.[4]

The beginnings of slavery had been part of the development of the Florida territory since the 1500s, when European explorers brought slaves to Pensacola. When Spain ruled the port settlement, the slaves had been allowed to serve on juries and to own property, but they had had to be under the guardianship of a European.[5] By the mid-1800s, cotton plantations that relied on slave labor had spread over several counties along the northern border of the Panhandle. In 1850, there were 336 slaves in Walton County.[6] By the time southern states talked of forming a separate government, more than 60,000 slaves were living in Florida, nearly half the total population of the state. About a third of the white residents claimed them as property.[7]

Long before the Civil War started, slavery had become a volatile issue in the region. An incident in Pensacola illustrates how deeply emotions were running some sixteen years before the war. This event riveted national attention on the port city and prompted an outcry by Frederick Douglass and other leading abolitionists.

Jonathan Walker, a white shipbuilder from Cape Cod, had moved in 1844 to Pensacola, where he worked at various jobs. His true mission, however, was to help fugitive slaves reach freedom by the Underground Railroad.[8]

He earned a reputation for treating black men as equals, eating meals with them at the same table.[9] Pensacola officials warned him that residents had angrily complained about his antislavery stand, and the city would not be able to protect him. But Walker would not be diverted from his goal of helping slaves.

Several slaves asked him to help them escape in June 1844. He told them to meet him at midnight at the beach.[10] Walker stocked his boat with water, bacon, and other supplies. That night, June 22, he pushed off with seven slaves aboard and headed for the British-ruled Bahamas. The group would not reach the islands.[11]

Walker had felt ill for a couple of days, and his condition worsened in the heat of the sun. He lay sick in the bottom of the boat. The slaves knew little of sailing, and the boat drifted. After fourteen days, a federal sloop spotted them and, suspecting something was out of the ordinary, towed them to Key West. Walker was charged with stealing slaves. His hands and feet were shackled in iron chains, and he was locked in the filthy hold of the steamboat *General Taylor* and taken to Pensacola.[12]

His bail was set at ten thousand dollars, a fortune in 1844. He had fifteen dollars. He was locked in an empty cell about fifteen feet square with a five-pound shackle around his ankle chaining him to the floor. Still sick, he lost weight, becoming as thin as a skeleton, as he wrote in a letter to his wife. For the first month, he slept on the damp floor of the cell until given straw to make a pallet.[13]

Spectators crowded the street when a deputy marshal, revolver drawn, escorted Walker to court. Walker was found guilty of stealing slaves and sentenced to seven years in prison, a year for each slave, and fined forty-two hundred dollars, six hundred per slave. He was taken outside, his head and hands were locked between two boards, and citizens pelted him with rotten eggs. Prison officials decided to brand the palm of his right hand with *SS* for "slave stealer." Although another man stepped up to the task, at least one courageous blacksmith refused to make the branding iron.[14]

Walker was chained in solitary confinement for three hundred days. Reversing the symbolism of Walker's scar, Frederick Douglass and other antislavery activists called Walker the "slave savior." The poet and reformer John Greenleaf Whittier penned a poem, "The Branded Hand," about the incident. "Then lift that manly right hand, bold ploughman of the wave!" wrote Whittier. "Its branded palm shall prophesy, 'Salvation to the Slave!'"

Finally, because of the national outcry, Walker was fined forty-five dollars and freed. He then wrote of the inhumane jail conditions and of slaves lashed with leather straps in a book published by the American Anti-Slavery Society in Boston.[15]

The controversy over slavery also created tension among residents of other areas of the Emerald Coast, where Northerners and Southerners lived side by side. In Walton County, the issue forced John Newton to choose between his ethics and his job as the schoolmaster of Knox Hill Academy near Eucheeanna.

Born in Pittsburgh, Pennsylvania, in 1814, Newton lost both his parents when he was at an early age. As he grew up, education became increasingly important to him, and he went to school while working various jobs. His determination resulted in a degree from the well-respected Amherst College in Massachusetts.[16] He developed a lifelong love for learning, which he wanted to share.

After teaching in several states, in 1848 he accepted the job of schoolmaster of Knox Hill Academy in east Walton County. A slender, slight man, he was known for few words but abundant integrity. The school earned a reputation for strict discipline and high academic standards.[17]

However, Newton began to rile some in the community when he spoke his mind about the ills of slavery. For a time, his views were tolerated: "At that day no other Northern man could have held and expressed his views on slavery as he did and be safe in this section," local historian John McKinnon wrote. But parents and school trustees became outraged when they discovered that Newton had added several books with an abolitionist slant to the school's bookshelves. Newton had gone too far in promoting his politics. The trustees called a special meeting.[18]

Newton declared that if the books went, he would go, too. After much agonizing, the trustees voted to ban the books. Newton resigned. He journeyed to California, then returned to Santa Rosa Sound, founding a settlement, Mary Esther, named for his two daughters. Knox Hill Academy hired other teachers, but the trustees eventually realized they had made a mistake in letting Newton go and hired him back. The job would not last long.[19]

When Abraham Lincoln was elected president in 1860, northwest Florida was just as caught up, and divided, by slavery as the rest of the country. By the Christmas holidays, following Lincoln's victory on November 6, secession flags were flying high. In Pensacola, secessionists stood on street corners and called for Florida to withdraw from the Union, while burning Lincoln in effigy.[20]

During the first week of 1861, sixty-nine delegates were meeting in Tallahassee at a special convention called to decide whether Florida would remain in the Union or pull out in rebellion.[21] Thus far, only South Carolina and Mississippi had seceded. The Confederate government had not yet been formed, and no one knew what would happen next.

At the same time, the Pensacola showdown that nearly started the war began building over control of three forts and a navy yard on Pensacola Bay. The servicemen stationed there would soon have to choose sides. Should they remain loyal to the United States or rebel and risk being charged with treason?

Company G of the 1st United States Artillery was stationed at barracks on the mainland between Fort Barrancas and the navy yard. First Lieutenant Adam Slemmer and Second Lieutenant J. H. Gilman, in command while the senior officers were on leave, heard rumors that Florida troops were preparing to seize the military posts.[22] The rumors were true. Governor Madison Perry had called for volunteers to join a state militia and had asked Alabama to send troops to help seize the forts. He was encouraged by the success of a small militia force that had captured an arsenal at Chattahoochee on the Apalachicola River where five hundred thousand rounds of musket ammunition and fifty thousand pounds of gunpowder were stored.[23]

In Pensacola, the second officer in command of Company G, Gilman, detailed the unfurling crisis in a report. He wrote that the federal soldiers began moving their gunpowder from an old Spanish fort to Fort Barrancas on January 8, 1861. At about midnight, a soldier standing guard thought he heard something. A party of twenty men was creeping up to the fort. "Halt," the guard called. When they failed to reply, he fired his musket, and the raiders fled.[24]

The next day, January 9, the federal posts received orders to prevent the military installations from being seized. Slemmer decided to consolidate federal forces at Fort Pickens on Santa Rosa Island. Commodore James Armstrong at the navy yard was reluctant to take any action. He was caught in the middle, torn between the Union officers who needed one of his ships to carry soldiers across the bay to Fort Pickens, and the secessionists, who insisted the navy yard should be state property.[25]

In Washington, James Buchanan, who was still president since Lincoln had not yet been inaugurated, prepared to send more troops to secure the forts. Emerald Coast settlers feared being caught in the middle of war. Meanwhile, delegates at the secession convention in Tallahassee approved a resolution by McQueen McIntosh of Apalachicola that gave the assembly the right to take Florida out of the Union.[26]

The next day, Thursday, January 10, while tensions escalated in Pensacola, visitors crowded into the galleries of the Senate Chamber. Delegates lobbied among themselves, tense voices pitched higher with excitement. "Every hour is important," Governor Madison Perry told the assembly. He read a telegram from Florida's congressmen in Washington reporting that federal troops were moving to seize Pensacola forts.[27]

Several delegates pleaded to at least postpone the vote until the bordering states of Georgia and Alabama decided whether to secede. Other amendments to delay action were submitted. One by one they were voted down. At noon the debating stopped. An ordinance declaring that Florida would immediately withdraw from the United States was read to a hushed assembly.[28]

In a landslide, sixty-two voted to become the third state to secede. Only seven delegates voted "nay." Two of them, McCaskill and Morrison, were from Walton County, earning it the nickname "Lincoln County."[29]

While the secession convention delegates were voting, Union officer Slemmer finally convinced the U.S. Navy's Commodore Armstrong to order the *Wyandotte* ship to carry eighty-one men to Fort Pickens.

Slemmer and Gilman warned their men to be ready to defend Fort Pickens against militiamen on the mainland. They hurriedly mounted guns at the old dilapidated fort, which had not been used since the Mexican War. Late in the afternoon on January 12, four men representing the governors of Florida and Alabama sailed to the fort and asked the Union officers to surrender their post peacefully.

"I am here by authority of the President of the United States, and I do not recognize the authority of any governor to demand the surrender of United States property,—a governor is nobody here," Slemmer told them, according to the report by Gilman.[30]

"On the 12th we saw the flag at the Navy Yard lowered, and then knew that it had been quietly and tamely surrendered," Gilman wrote. "Seeing our flag thus lowered to an enemy caused intense excitement and emotion, a mingled feeling of shame, anger and defiance. Not yet having a flag-staff up, we hung our flag over the north-west bastion of the fort, that all might see 'that our flag was still there.'"[31]

Tension mounted. Enemy lines were drawn. At Fort Pickens, the soldiers ached with exhaustion. During daylight, they worked to restore the post and prepare their guns. At night, they stayed awake to keep watch for an attack. In fact an attack did occur. On the night of January 13, they exchanged fire with a small group of fighters from shore, but there were no casualties.

Two days later, militia officers from the mainland crossed the bay again and asked Slemmer to surrender. Colonel W. H. Chase, a retired U.S. Army officer appointed commander of the Florida troops, began reading the request. His eyes filled with tears and his voice choked. Slemmer again refused to give up the fort.[32]

Mississippi senator Jefferson Davis and Florida congressmen telegraphed the Confederate troops on the mainland, urging them to avoid bloodshed. A truce was declared, but Pensacola nevertheless was in a state of war.[33]

The Confederate States of America was formed on February 4, 1861, and began calling for troops. After Lincoln took office March 4, he declared a blockade of Southern ports, and forty-two navy ships began maneuvering into position, while another 222 were being built.[34] On April 12, shots were fired at Fort Sumpter. Lincoln called for troops to suppress the Confederacy.

The Union gunboat USS *Water Witch* anchored offshore near East Pass.[35] At Pensacola, reinforcements boosted the numbers of fighters on both sides of the bay, and during the war the port would become the largest city in Florida.

14. On September 13, 1861, in one of the first naval battles of the Civil War, Union troops burned the Confederate schooner *Judah* in Pensacola harbor. Courtesy of State Archives of Florida.

The first instance of bloodshed in Florida occurred there in September. A federal gunboat, the *Colorado,* sailed to the navy yard and attacked a Confederate ship, the *Judah.* Three Union soldiers were killed. There were no Confederate losses recorded.[36]

In retaliation, Confederate troops attacked Union camps on Santa Rosa Island on October 9. Fighting hand to hand, the raiders torched the camp. Both sides suffered losses—fourteen Union soldiers and twenty-eight Confederate soldiers were killed.[37]

On November 22, soldiers at Fort Pickens and troops aboard two Union battleships, the *Niagara* and the *Richmond,* bombarded Fort McRee, which Confederate forces held at the eastern end of Perdido Key. For two days they fought, with several casualties on each side. The communities of Warrington and Wolsey near Pensacola burned as well as a building at the navy yard, which produced ammunition for Confederate troops. Fort McRee was heavily damaged.[38]

At Camp Walton, Emerald Coast soldiers restlessly tried to fill the days. During their idle hours, John McKinnon and others realized the "hills" where their camp was located were mounds of dirt that were so symmetrical they

15. *Harper's Weekly* depicted Union and Confederate troops during an 1861 skirmish at Pensacola harbor. Courtesy of State Archives of Florida.

must have been built by men instead of being formed by nature. They started digging with picks and shovels. At barely more than a spade's length deep, they came to human bones and pottery relics. The Confederate soldiers had discovered a ceremonial mound built by men who had lived on the sound between AD 800 and 1400. The mound was near where the Indian Temple Mound Museum is now located.[39]

Word reached Camp Walton that Union troops from a federal gunboat were landing at East Pass. Captain McPherson sent a scouting team by boat to Joe's Bayou then on foot to a bluff overlooking the pass. They crouched behind scrub and watched two Union landing boats approach. The Walton Guard soldiers opened fire when the small boats came within 150 yards. Reports vary about how many Union casualties there were, but by one account two were killed and two were wounded. When the gunboat returned fire, the Walton Guards retreated to Joe's Bayou and then sailed to Camp Walton. They suffered no casualties.

The Union gunboat sailed to Camp Walton to retaliate. The Confederate supply boat *Lady of the Lake* was a sitting duck stranded with no wind. The Union boat fired twenty-one shots at the Confederate schooner. Finally a breeze took her out of range.[40]

A Christmas party with 120 girls lifted the spirits of the Walton Guard soldiers as described in a letter dated December 29, 1861, by Alexander McDonald to his cousin Duncan McDonald: "The funniest thing that happened was after the party broke up at number 3." He explained, "it was Miss Nancy kissed Danield Moore. They looked like two Kitens [*sic*] a playin when they went to kiss."[41]

The slack time ended, however, in the spring. In April 1862, federal soldiers led by Captain Henry W. Closson marched down Santa Rosa Island from Pensacola. Across Santa Rosa Sound from Camp Walton they opened fire just as the Walton Guard soldiers were waking up: "I think there were at least 4 or 5 hundred men," wrote a John L. in a letter to Knox Hill schoolmaster Newton from Boggy Bayou on April 2, 1862.[42] The Walton Guard hurriedly ran away, with no deaths reported, and retreated to Boggy Bayou for a few weeks.

Bands of renegades roamed the state, murdering anyone thought to be an abolitionist, burning homes and stealing crops and animals. The renegades brought a "reign of terror" to Florida, wrote correspondents with the *New York Times* and the *New York Tribune*. On the Emerald Coast, seven people who lived in Walton County were lynched for pro-Union sentiments, and hounds were unleashed on a woman who refused to give information, killing her.[43]

16. Confederate canons line Pensacola harbor in 1861. Courtesy of State Archives of Florida.

Residents who had moved to Florida from the north also felt the brunt of wartime emotions. Leonard Destin and his family were taken inland to an internment camp at Freeport to make sure that he could not aid Union gunboats anchored offshore.[44]

In the civilian world, the war promoted an atmosphere of distrust and violence. At Knox Hill Academy, the war was taking its toll on schoolmaster Newton. He hated to see his students leave school only to possibly die for a cause that he believed was wrong. As the war provoked bitterness between Southerners and Northerners in the community, he became dispirited and left the school again.

From California in 1864, Newton wrote to his sisters asking for news of soldiers from the Euchee Valley: "I still think and more strongly than ever that the Confederacy will never gain," he wrote. "But O what loss of life, & limb, & property. Fla. always was a poor country, but now, & for many years after the war will be worse & worse. Here we do not feel the effects of the war any more than if it were in a foreign country." Newton would long feel estranged from the people of the Florida community. On September 28, 1868,

17. The Confederate 9th Mississippi unit camp at Pensacola in 1861. Photo by J. D. Edwards. Courtesy of State Archives of Florida.

18. Confederate soldiers take over Pensacola Harbor in 1861 after Union troops moved across the bay to Fort Pickens. Photo by J. D. Edwards. Courtesy of State Archives of Florida.

he wrote to someone named Daniel, "Let me know how you get along. You need not be careful to convey any information to *anyone about me*. . . . There is no one who is really my . . . friend . . . excepting my own household. If the people about Knox Hill can live without me I can without them. I have *wasted* a large portion of my life with them."[45]

Confederate forces at Pensacola grew to more than three thousand men.[46] But the numbers soon dwindled as companies were called to battlefields in Tennessee and other states. West Florida militia groups were called by the Confederacy to form the First Florida Infantry. The Walton Guard became Companies D and E while the Pensacola Guards formed Company K.[47] Both groups were short of clothes, guns, and ammunition, prompting citizens to organize the Pensacola Committee of Relief to provide weapons and supplies.[48]

Eventually the Confederates pulled out of the port city, as did all but forty adult civilians. Confederate troops destroyed factories, boats, and whatever else they could not carry so that goods and resources would not fall into Union hands. Flames consumed the town.[49] Companies of the First Infantry went on to fight in battles at Lookout Mountain, Tennessee, Perryville, Kentucky, and Chickamauga, Kennesaw Mountain, and Atlanta. Pensacola fell to Union control and was occupied by federal troops.

Union troops mounted attacks on coastal areas, but as Shelby Foote characterized them, they were merely nibbling "at the rim of the rebellion."[50] One Union tactic focused on the inland Emerald Coast region. In September 1864, Union troops began marching from Pensacola to the interior to cut off Confederate supplies of beef, salt, and cotton as well as to get food for their own troops.

On September 18, Brigadier General Alexander Asboth led seven hundred men on horseback to East Pass, where they got food and supplies from a steamer, the *Lizzie Davis*. Then they headed northeast through Walton County. At dawn on September 23, they galloped into Eucheeanna, where they ransacked houses, rounded up horses, and took fifteen prisoners. On the Choctawhatchee River, they destroyed Douglas's Ferry and small boats and rounded up cattle from surrounding farms.

Asboth's troops next rode east to Marianna, the headquarters of Confederate forces in west Florida, about fifty miles away in Jackson County. They broke through a barricade of boys and elderly men called the "Cradle and Grave Company," a force variously reported as numbering from fifty to three hundred. The raiders shot young snipers in the windows of an Episcopal church and then set fire to the building. At a nearby river, the Marianna fighters held off the cavalry, which then turned back and plundered the town. When the Union soldiers finally rode out of town, they took eighty-one prisoners, four hundred cows, and two hundred horses—and six hundred freed slaves. Casualties totaled fifteen federal soldiers by one report, and thirty-nine by another, and five to nine Marianna fighters. Asboth was wounded in the face and left arm.[51]

The Union soldiers returned to Point Washington on Choctawhatchee Bay, where the wounded boarded the *Lizzie Davis* bound for Pensacola. The raid on west Florida had lasted sixteen days.[52]

Drifters and draft dodgers wandered throughout the state. Women struggled to tend crops and to manage without supplies barred by the Union blockade at the bays of Pensacola, Choctawhatchee, and St. Andrews. Cattle that had not been seized by Union soldiers were taken to feed Confederate troops, or if herded to market were likely to be stolen by deserters.

At one point during the war, General Asboth notified federal officials that two hundred starving refugee women and children had arrived at East Pass. Thousands of people left their homes when they could not make a living with the man of the house off at war or when Union troops marched into their area according to historian George F. Pearce.

Some settlers made money and helped the Confederate cause as blockade-runners, sneaking their small boats around enemy ships, through waterways too numerous for the federal navy to guard. Sailing cotton and other goods to Caribbean ports, "the smugglers operated out of nearly every bay and inlet in the state," according to Mark Derr. One smuggling point was on the west end of Choctawhatchee Bay. Confederates fended off at least one attack there by a troop of Vermont soldiers who tried to capture the blockade-runner *Champion*.[53]

Union troops built barracks on Hurricane Island at the entrance to St. Andrews Bay, where they tried to guard against blockade-runners. Union gunboats patrolled the waters but were largely unsuccessful because the sprawling bay was so large. However, Union soldiers occasionally fired on Confederates, and they built a small prison at Redfish Point for those they did manage to catch.

At the town of St. Andrews, Confederates were loading several boats with cotton to ship out when the Union *Roebuck* crew came ashore to get water from a spring. Several soldiers were killed.[54] After one skirmish, Union casualties were buried on Hurricane Island.[55] In another incident, in Millville, federal gunboats seized the schooner *Kim*, capturing a cargo of tobacco, cotton, and twenty thousand dollars in Confederate money. During one exchange of gunfire, all thirty-two buildings of St. Andrews were destroyed.[56]

Up and down the coast, hundreds of big iron kettles dotted the white sandy shore. Seawater was boiled in them to get salt, which was so essential in preserving meat and fish that salt suppliers were exempt from the Confederate draft and from paying taxes. The industry employed some five thousand men. As valuable as bullets, salt skyrocketed from a penny a pound to five dollars a pound during the war.[57]

Hundreds of salt operations circled St. Andrews Bay, making the area one of the largest producers of salt in the South, turning out four thousand bushels a day.[58] Smoke clouded the sky at St. Andrews Bay in 1863 when a Union ship shelled nearly three hundred saltworks and destroyed much of the Confederate supply by dumping sand into the salt. They destroyed tubs, pumps, and other equipment to try to shut down the operations. Soon after, however, the saltworks started up again. The salt was hauled by mule-drawn wagons to Montgomery or by barge to other ports.[59]

Nearly five years to the day after the war started, news slowly spread through the Emerald Coast that Robert E. Lee had surrendered to Ulysses S. Grant on April 9. Tallahassee was the only capital east of the Mississippi that had remained under Confederate control.[60] In the homes of the Destins, the McKinnons, and all the other families throughout the Emerald Coast, relief that the killing was over was mixed with apprehension about the future of a state on the losing side. They had barely taken in the news when, less than a week later, they learned President Lincoln had been shot on Good Friday by John Wilkes Booth during a performance at Ford's Theatre in Washington, D.C.

Soldiers came home to the Emerald Coast, some wounded, all of them scarred by the horrors of war, overwhelmed to see fields of weeds and empty pastures. There are conflicting reports about how many of the original Walton Guard returned. By one account, nearly half of the sixty men who initially signed up were killed—among the six hundred thousand casualties nation-wide. Several members of the Walton Guard walked out of a Union prison at Johnson's Island, near Sandusky, Ohio. Leonard Destin and his family were freed from the internment camp at Freeport and went home to East Pass.

These bruised Emerald Coast families would try to put their homesteads back together as the country doctored wounds of a nation nearly destroyed. The story of a young widow who moved with her two young sons to an uncle's orange grove on the Florida frontier illustrates postwar life in the Panhandle. The writer Jane R. Griffing told of meeting the widow, whom she did not identify in her 1883 letters. The widow had remarried. "Two children were born and died," Griffing wrote. "There was no society, no medical attendance or nursing when ill, no servants to do the work." Griffing continued the litany of the woman's hardships: "No proper food, no comforts, nothing but hard work when she could stand on her feet. . . . Her delicate beauty faded in the hard, rough life."[61]

A former correspondent with the *Chicago Times,* while riding a train through northwest Florida, saw from his window that the war had turned white-tufted cotton fields into miles of neglected land. The writer, George M.

Barbour, observed that the farmland looked as though it had "suddenly been arrested in its growth, and was in a state of suspended animation." He had visited the state while covering a trip by General Grant and had liked it so much that he moved to Florida after the war. While riding the Florida Central Railroad from Jacksonville, heading toward Pensacola, he learned that many of the people living there were in fact from the north.[62]

Towns along the way were "quaint, old-fashioned" clusters of faded brick buildings centered around squares shaded by oaks, circled by pumps, with water troughs and "the universal southern hitching-rail on high posts, with always a number of saddle mules and horses attached." Some communities wore an "unmistakable mantle of mildewy decay, of neglect rapidly verging on dilapidation. . . . The suburbs make an impression altogether more favorable," he wrote. Handsome houses with families sitting on verandas stood along shaded sidewalks, with "The Pirates of Penzance" and other tunes "floating through the open windows, from the keys of skillfully played pianos."

Admiring fields, forests, plantations, and pastures where cattle grazed, he remarked on the bitterness of many in Florida over losing the war, but he was hopeful that anti-abolitionist attitudes would end with the next generation. "At present the goodly people are 'brooding upon memories,'" he wrote.

When the train stopped at the hamlet of Chattahoochee, the writer got off and climbed into a stagecoach that took him first to Marianna, then west across Walton and Okaloosa counties to Pensacola. "The ride was tedious and fatiguing, but not really monotonous, for the scenery was very attractive, except in occasional tracts. Vernon, Euchee Anna, and Milton, passed *en route*, are all three countyseats, and are small, drowsy-looking towns, old-fashioned. . . . A square, an old-fashioned tavern, a court-house, and a few shops, may be said to compose each and all of them."

The area desperately needed to complete rail lines, he said, blaming money-eyed special-interest groups such as lawyers for delaying construction.

Barbour arrived in Pensacola in the spring of 1880. He quoted a local handbook about the city as saying the Escambia River offered superb freshwater fishing for trout, bass, pike, and bream. A good angler could catch fifty fish an hour. The bay was loaded with saltwater fish, which, at fifty cents for half a dozen Spanish mackerel, were much cheaper than in the North.

"No one can claim to have seen what fishing is until he has visited the snapper banks off Santa Rosa Island," said the guidebook. "There the famous red snapper can be caught, two at a time, weighing from five pounds to sixty, as rapidly as the line is thrown in." A fisherman's catch was limited only by his endurance.

Barbour learned how to look for "turtle crawls" on Santa Rosa Island, where turtles' shells had dragged across the sand when they came ashore to lay eggs. He read that thousands of alligators could be found at Sabine Pass. Bathhouses stood on the banks of the bay. He also saw the ruins of Fort McRee.

He described the city of Pensacola as being charming and clean, with nicely laid-out streets. It had been rebuilt after the war, and the ghost town had come to life again. The population in 1880 had climbed to 6,845[63]—and the population would soar even more in the once-deserted streets during a lumber and shipping boom over the next two decades.

Places to Visit

The Civil War Soldiers Museum, 108 South Palafox Place, Pensacola.

Cannon at Indian Temple Mound Museum, Fort Walton Beach.

Books to Read

Blockaders, Refuges, and Contrabands: Civil War on Florida's Gulf Coast, 1861–1865, by George E. Buker (Tuscaloosa: University of Alabama Press, 1993).

Pensacola during the Civil War: A Thorn in the Side of the Confederacy, by George F. Pearce (Gainesville: University Press of Florida, 2000).

6. Sawmills and Turpentine Stills

Driving down a lane flanked by magnolias and five-hundred-year-old oaks, a former reporter at the *New York World Telegram* came to a two-story house with plantation porches, scarred by peeling paint and nearly hidden by scrub and Spanish moss.[1] The setting could have been in a movie. Later, it was.

Lois Maxon was on a Sunday drive with a friend that day in 1963 when she discovered the vacant house, which had been built by William Henry Wesley at the height of the timber industry in 1897. The two-story Greek revival house was nearly identical to a plantation mansion, Dunleith, in Natchez, Mississippi, that Wesley might have seen during the Civil War.[2]

Miss Maxon peeped through dirty panes of windows nearly as tall as the thirteen-foot ceilings. The windows were designed to pull in breezes off nearby Choctawhatchee Bay. Large rooms opening off a central hall could nicely showcase the heirlooms of her family, which owned Maxon manufacturing company in Muncie, Indiana.

She walked across the twelve-acre estate, following a trail to the marshy bank of Tucker Bayou, where the southeast side of Choctawhatchee Bay ends at Point Washington. She saw little left of the once-thriving Strickland and Wesley Lumber Company.

Miss Maxon bought the seven-bedroom, one-bath house. She hired designers to restore the home and gardens, and she filled the newly painted and papered rooms with antiques. From France came Louis VI chairs and a settee for the drawing room; from Italy, Empire period pieces for the dining room; from Turkey, an 1880 rocker for the library.

Five years later, she became ill and donated the estate and the antiques to Florida. The state opened the house to visitors and named the site Eden Gardens State Park. The property on the remote, sultry bayou provided an eerie backdrop in 1972 for a horror movie, *Frogs,* which starred Ray Milland.[3]

The backwater site of lush marshes and towering oaks at Tucker Bayou had offered Wesley more than a scenic backdrop for his stately house. The bayou

19. Lois Maxon discovered a vacated antebellum house, beautiful but in need of repairs, on a Sunday drive in 1963 near Point Washington. The site later became Eden State Gardens. Photo by Jean Lufkin Bouler.

provided the water transportation crucial for the lumber company he built. His operation tapped into a lucrative market fueled by rebuilding after the American Civil War and the Franco-Prussian War in Europe.[4] Wesley realized that the virgin forests of the Emerald Coast could feed that appetite for wood.

The Strickland and Wesley Lumber Company supported a turn-of-the-century community. Twenty small houses were built for laborers, and a commissary stocked goods for them. The heart of the operation was a sawmill, planer mill, and dry kiln that stood next to a dock extending beyond the tall marsh grasses into open water.[5] Around the bay, logs were lashed together as rafts and floated down creeks and rivers to the mills. After being sawn and planed into boards, the lumber was stacked on barges that glided into the bay and on to port in Pensacola, where schooners took the lumber to the north or west, or to Europe or South America.

Fire destroyed the mill twice, and Wesley rebuilt it each time. But the third time flames raced through the mill, the Strickland and Wesley Lumber Company folded.[6] Broken pilings poking out of the water are the only reminders of the lumber operation that hummed on the now-quiet bayou.

Other lumber mills circled Choctawhatchee Bay. Forests in many southern states had been depleted before the Civil War, cut for lumber and slashed for turpentine. Loggers and turpentine distillers moved southward, gobbling trees along the way.

Loggers like George Oglesby from Georgia carved out settlements in the backwoods. Many newcomers took advantage of the Federal Homestead Act of 1862, under which a family could get 160 to 320 acres by settling on it for five years. Families camped until they could build a cabin in this frontier. They often leased their land to timber and turpentine companies.[7]

Longleaf pines covered thousands of acres. They were irresistible to the postwar merchants craving lumber and turpentine. "No country affords more or better wood, liveoak, cedar, cypress, yellow pine," marveled naturalist Bernard Romans, who had traveled through the area a hundred years earlier, in 1776: "The superior quality of West Florida timber stands acknowledged without a rival." He cautioned that the timber industry should be regulated to prevent waste.[8] More than a century would pass before government officials would take that step.

Making money from trees was grueling work in virgin forests and swamps that harbored deadly rattlesnakes, cottonmouth moccasins, panthers, bears, and malaria-carrying mosquitoes. Logging was slow and tedious. Instead of cutting trees at their base, some loggers cut them waist-high so they wouldn't have to bend over. The ugly stumps spoiled the once-forested landscape.

Bringing down a hundred-foot pine was just the beginning. After its branches were sheared, the log had to be balanced on a cart outfitted with huge wooden wheels taller than a man. A team of six to eight oxen, their grooved hooves steady in mud, pulled logs to the nearest creek or river. Logs were floated downstream to bayside docks. The so-called sticks were bound with chains into rafts of five hundred and towed to Point Washington and other mills on the Choctawhatchee Bay and its tributaries.[9] Steam-powered saws whined on the banks of the bay.

At Fourmile Creek near Freeport, warehouses lined the bank where boats docked so the timber could be loaded and hauled to Pensacola. In the harbor of the bustling port city of Pensacola, scores of square-rigged sailing ships anchored, waiting to fill their holds with wood they would carry on to other ports.[10]

Pensacola became a boomtown after the Civil War when the Florida legislature granted millions of acres in right-of-way for railroad tracks. The

20. Log trains steamed through vast pine forests throughout the Emerald Coast. In the late 1800s and early 1900s, logging became an economic mainstay. Courtesy of Special Collections, University of West Florida Library, Pensacola.

Pensacola and Atlantic Railroad connected sawmills throughout the Emerald Coast to Pensacola's port, which in turn supplied markets on the Atlantic seaboard.[11] International trade brought Greeks, Germans, Italians, and Norwegians to the town, and they settled in neighborhoods near their churches or synagogues.[12]

A key figure in Pensacola during the 1870s and 1880s was William Chipley, a railroad baron who was called "Mr. Railroad of West Florida."[13] Born in Columbus, Georgia, he had served as a lieutenant colonel in the Confederate army, was wounded twice, captured, and imprisoned.[14] As a railroad czar and chairman of the state Democratic Executive Committee, he wielded considerable political power. Chipley's political machine clashed with liberals over land grants that settlers wanted to homestead and over freight rates. Chipley later ran for the U.S. Senate but lost in a bitter campaign.[15]

However, his mark on Pensacola was significant. He invested railroad money in banks, wharves, and warehouses. By the late 1800s, Pensacola was bustling with business. Two-thousand-foot wharfs loaded with lumber from the numerous mills throughout northwest Florida reached into the bay.[16]

Eleven sawmills operated in the city alone. Seventeen tugboats carried planks to the many schooners from all over the world that were anchored in the bay.[17] The complexion of the city changed from a military post to thriving seaport.

Quarantine stations were set up to inspect ships for signs of yellow fever because health officials believed contaminated ships started epidemics.[18] The city was quarantined several times during the 1870s. Hospital care cost up to $1.90 a day, and a burial cost $10.00.[19]

The development of refrigerated railcars in the 1860s meant that fresh fish could be shipped north. Two of the largest companies in Pensacola were the E. E. Saunders Company and the Warren Fish Company, which shipped more than three million pounds of fish a year by rail, much of it from the Emerald Coast.[20]

When Geronimo, chief of the Apaches, was jailed at Fort Pickens, residents flocked to see him. For entertainment, the city proudly opened an opera house in 1883, which drew Shakespeare performances and such entertainers as Sarah Bernhardt.[21]

At the eastern end of the Emerald Coast, communities also thrived as the timber business spurred development around St. Andrews Bay. Many of those communities later became incorporated as Panama City. Brothers James and Harry Watson built a lumber company on a site that would be called Millville

21. Leonard Destin and other Emerald Coast fishermen hauled their catch to Saunders fish house on Pensacola Bay. Courtesy of State Archives of Florida.

22. Sawdust covered every surface in this sawmill in Pensacola. Photo by John A. Walker. Courtesy of State Archives of Florida.

and supplied timbers for railroad trestles for the Pensacola and Atlantic Railroad.[22]

The largest sawmill in the area was the German-American Lumber Company, which owned two hundred thousand acres in Millville and at one time employed three hundred workers.[23] The company built a rail line to area logging camps. A French-Canadian, Henry Bovis, had built the mill and later sold it to a German syndicate. During World War I, the federal government seized the mill, fearing the Germans were going to make the site an enemy base. The United States also interred a German company executive at Fort Oglethorpe in Atlanta until after the war, when he returned to Germany.[24]

Lumber was not the only product of the Emerald Coast forests. The pines of the Panhandle also yielded resin, which could be used to make turpentine. As far back as the fifteenth century, shipbuilders sealed hulls with pine gum. Carpenters and potters used resin to glue wood and to seal clay vessels. By the 1880s, demand skyrocketed as turpentine was used in a host of household products including soap, ink, rubber, paint, medicine, hair spray, and cosmetics.[25] The booming industry provided another economic mainstay for the Emerald Coast. The Metts, Garniers, and Faircloth turpentine companies were among many in the area. A typical operation might be like that of

23. A Pensacola lumberyard and sawmill. The industry provided jobs but ravaged forests. Early developers bypassed the Emerald Coast's stump-studded landscape and instead built resorts in south Florida. Courtesy of Special Collections, University of West Florida Library, Pensacola.

24. Thousands of feet of Emerald Coast timber were loaded into sailing ships at Pensacola for shipment to Europe and the northern United States. Courtesy of Special Collections, University of West Florida Library, Pensacola.

25. Teams of oxen pulled logs to numerous sawmills like this one near Pensacola in 1925. Courtesy of State Archives of Florida.

D. Faircloth, which consisted of a twenty-five-barrel still, one hundred dip barrels, seven mules, one horse, three wagons, a hundred thousand boxes, and a host of tools.[26]

Turpentiners typically leased land for two to six years. They burned the understory brush each winter to prevent major fires and to nourish the trees.[27]

The business was a harsh one. Turpentine laborers were often former slaves who could get no other work or black prisoners leased to companies by the state. From March until November, crews were hauled to the woods to drain gum from pines.[28] They worked from dawn to dusk. Each man was responsible for a tract of two thousand pines. Crewmen had specialized jobs of cutting, attaching cups, or dipping.[29]

A worker used a long-handled ax to slash as high up the tree trunk as he could and scraped a section of bark down to his waist. He "wounded" the pine by chipping its trunk along the skinned part to make the sap ooze. At the base of the wound, the worker slashed a "box" nearly a foot wide and five or so inches deep into the trunk to catch and hold the flow of resin.[30] A skilled man could chop ninety boxes a day. Metal or clay cups were later used to collect the gum, and these were placed a few feet higher every year. The tree bled for two to four weeks.[31] Then a worker dipped a couple of pints of gum per tree with an iron ladle or tupelo spoon.[32] Crewmen then cut fresh streaks into the trunks so the trees would bleed more gum.[33]

The sticky gum was dipped into barrels, which were hauled to the still by teams of four mules. Then the gum was poured into copper kettles over a fire and cooked for two hours.[34] A boilerman adjusted the temperature of a mixture of water and resin by listening to whether it bubbled, making sure the mixture did not get so hot it would explode. Steam flowed through a copper pipe into a cooling tub, where it liquefied into turpentine.[35]

Workers lived in camps of shanties that barely provided shelter. Their daily pay depended on the skill performed, ranging from only seventy-five cents for cup installers to four dollars for dippers—poverty wages even then. The men had to buy all of their food, clothes, and supplies from the company store, often at inflated prices and on credit.[36] Too poor to pay off their debt, they were locked into the system—"slavery in modern clothing," wrote Stetson Kennedy.[37]

In Bay County, some turpentine still owners leased convicts from the state for $150 each per year. The prisoners' ankles were chained while they worked to keep them from running away. They were beaten at night if they failed to dip their quota of resin that day.[38]

26. Businesses lined Pensacola harbor where hundreds of sailing ships arrived to load timber. The Civil War and the Franco-Prussian War in Europe created a huge demand for lumber. Courtesy of Special Collections, University of West Florida Library, Pensacola.

27. Turpentiners slashed pines for gum that was used in a host of products ranging from paint to hair spray. Courtesy of State Archives of Florida.

As the timber and turpentine boom peaked on the Emerald Coast, forests were ravaged by the unregulated industry. The technique of bleeding gum killed the trees in three to twelve years. When forests were used up, loggers and turpentiners moved on, leaving behind deserted villages and ugly stubble where grand virgin forests once stood. Clear-cutting longleaf pine forests radically reduced habitats for wolves, panthers, bears, red-cockaded woodpeckers, and gopher tortoises, which all became rare.[39]

Federal officials became concerned and decided to try to save the trees by designating thousands of acres as a national forest, the first one east of the Mississippi. In 1908, President Theodore Roosevelt established the Choctawhatchee National Forest, now part of Eglin Air Force Base, which has protected vast stands of trees.[40]

Inman F. Eldredge was named supervisor of the forest. He had served for six years under the chief forester in the Department of Agriculture, Gifford Pinchot, who was a friend of Roosevelt's. Eldredge named his headquarters for Pinchot, the conservationist he had admired. Eldredge earned only one thousand dollars a year, but he loved his work. Under his leadership, researchers used the national forest to experiment with better methods of forestry and turpentine gathering, borrowing ideas from France that would be less damaging to the pines. Those measures included shallower chipping and fewer cups per tree.[41]

By World War I, forests were depleted and tung oil and other materials were replacing resin in products. Tree farmers planted pulp pines for paper manufacturing instead of using slow-growing longleaf pines.[42] Operators closed their businesses; the lumber and turpentine boom ended. New industrial methods of extracting gum through a chemical process replaced turpentine camps. Pensacola, as well as small communities on the Emerald Coast, faced an economic crisis.[43]

While the timber and turpentine industries had brought workers and settlements into the interior of the area, much of the Emerald Coast remained isolated. Settlements such as Leonard Destin's fishing camp were nearly surrounded by the Gulf and Choctawhatchee Bay and could still be reached only by sand trails and boats. However, the Pensacola and Atlantic Railroad,

28. In the turpentine stills, boilermen had to get the temperature of the resin mixture just right in order to avoid an explosion. Courtesy of State Archives of Florida.

which laid tracks across the Panhandle for the logging industry, would for-ever change the character of the area.

Northerners began to discover other areas of Florida as an exotic land. But the Panhandle was unattractive to resort developers because clear-cutting had left a largely desolate landscape.[44] However, one hamlet was an exception that would affect much of the Emerald Coast.

Places to Visit

Replica of turpentine still, St. Andrews State Recreation Area, three miles east of Panama City off County Road 392 (Thomas Drive).

Eden Gardens State Park, Point Washington. From U.S. Highway 98, north on County Road 395, watch for entry lane on left.

Heritage Museum of Northwest Florida, 115 Westview Avenue, Valparaiso.

Historic Pensacola Village, 205 East Zaragoza Street, Pensacola.

Books to Read

Along the Bay: A Pictorial History of Bay County, by Marlene Womack (Norfolk, Va.: Pictorial Heritage Publishing, sponsored by Junior Service League of Panama City, 1994).

The Bay Country of Northwest Florida, by Marlene Womack (Apalachicola, Fla.: New Hope Press, 1998).

The History of Bay County: From the Beginning, by Tommy Smith (Panama City, Fla.: Bene/Mac Publishing, 2000).

Spirits of Turpentine: A History of Florida Naval Stores 1528–1950, by Robert S. Blount (Tallahassee: Florida Agricultural Museum, 1993).

7. Railroads: Gateway to the Gulf

In August 1884, a group of powerful men, wearing top hats and waistcoats, strode into the Hotel Athenaeum and planned an event that would bring thousands of visitors to the remote reaches of the Emerald Coast.[1]

The hotel stood in a hamlet, originally called Open Pond, which was little more than a train depot in the north Walton County frontier known mostly to Native Americans and Scottish pioneers. It seemed an unlikely place for railroad executives and entrepreneurs to meet.

A few years earlier, a surveying crew for the Pensacola and Atlantic Railroad led by William Dudley Chipley of Pensacola trekked through the area, plotting the route for trains. On a May day in 1881, Chipley came to a round, spring-fed lake surrounded by longleaf yellow pines and fell in love with the spot.[2] As Chipley camped on the shady banks, he envisioned a quaint town in the tranquil setting.

The tracks of the railroad, connecting the Panhandle to the Atlantic seaboard and the Midwest, were laid with strict instructions from Chipley not to disturb the beauty of the lake. A depot was built, and the hamlet was named Lake DeFuniak, for railroad executive Fred R. de Funiak.[3]

It is not known whether de Funiak ever came to the area, but his descendants have visited.[4] His father was a French count and his mother was Austrian. After spending part of his youth in Rome, he attended engineering school in Austria and worked as a railroad engineer in Egypt. After the Civil War, de Funiak worked his way up to chief engineer and general manager of the Louisville and Nashville Railway, which built the Pensacola and Atlantic portion through the Panhandle. He is said to have won a coin toss or roll of the dice to have the new town named for him.[5]

Like a magnet, the DeFuniak station pulled families from Eucheeanna and other settlements. Murray Cawthon came with his wife and nine children. They built the first store while living in a tent. J. C. Garrett built the first house. Dan L. Campbell built a drugstore. Carpenter Thompson put up a two-story wooden building that housed church services upstairs and a school downstairs. A barbershop was set up in a tent. A town was born.[6]

Located midway between Pensacola and Tallahassee, DeFuniak appealed to investors as an ideal site to develop a resort. On a plateau three hundred feet above sea level, the higher elevation reduced the risk of malaria, while springs constantly flowing from the limestone aquifer provided a healthy water supply.[7]

Chipley and several others, including investors from Iowa and Nebraska, formed the Lake DeFuniak Land Company. Within a few years, the county seat would be moved from Eucheeanna to DeFuniak, making the town the hub of the area.

The businessmen meeting at the Hotel Athenaeum touted the location, clean air, and spring water to try to convince the famous New York Chautauqua organization to hold a winter session of its weeks-long series of lectures, concerts, and social activities at the Walton County community. An Ohio manufacturer and a Pennsylvania minister had started Chautauqua in the 1870s as a summer educational program for Sunday school teachers. The New York event offered mental stimulation and social bonding, with an international mix of people and ideas. The festival was especially appealing after the killing and divisiveness of the recent Civil War. Gradually, the program had expanded into a cultural camp at Lake Chautauqua, New York, supplemented by year-round home study courses, local reading groups, and a book club.[8]

A winter session in the southern warmth would further expand the Chautauqua, and the DeFuniak group convinced one of the founders, Dr. A. H. Gillett, that the picturesque lake site would be perfect for a Florida Chautauqua.[9]

The men gathered at the Hotel Athenaeum that day in 1884 were working out details, hoping the Chautauqua would provide a national market for the resort. There was a sense of urgency in the air. There was much to be done to get ready.

Officers and advisors for the Florida Chautauqua came from all over the map. Alabama "Iron King" and railroad investor J. W. Sloss served as president.[10] Advisory board members were from Boston, Philadelphia, and Louisville, as well as cities in Wisconsin, Minnesota, and Georgia.

To promote the event, two hundred thousand pamphlets advertising "A

29. Program of the 1885
Florida Chautauqua
at DeFuniak Springs,
which was advertised
throughout the country.
Courtesy of State
Archives of Florida.

Winter Assembly in the Land of Summer" were printed. A quarterly newspaper was published in Cincinnati and distributed in other cities.[11] Getting the little settlement ready for the Chautauqua, slated to begin in just five months on February 10, 1885, must have been like preparing Atlanta for the 1996 Olympics. Artists, scholars, ministers, and musicians had to be scheduled. A seventy-room hotel—with indoor plumbing—had to be finished. Buildings or tents for meetings, sermons, and concerts had to be completed.

A master site plan showed the central lake circled by a park and adjoining streets that formed a wheel with avenues radiating like spokes.[12] The name of the town was changed to DeFuniak Springs to evoke more of a vacation air.

Promoters scheduled and advertised special train excursions. Round trip fares cost $30.55 from Cincinnati, $29.25 from Louisville, and $3.20 from Pensacola. The event was so popular that two trains ran daily from Chicago and St. Louis. Saturday excursions, such as one from Pensacola for one dollar, were available for day visitors.[13]

The planners anticipated a large crowd. If all the hotel rooms were rented—at rates of ten to fifteen dollars per week—then tents with wooden floors would be provided. Lumber would be available at six to eight dollars per thousand feet to build temporary huts, and pullman cars with sleeping compartments would be parked by the station for rent by the week.[14]

That autumn, the sound of hammering echoed across the lake as carpenters rushed to finish framing a wide veranda on the new Victorian-style Hotel Chautauqua. Workers nailed clapboards on a "Tabernacle" and painted new picket fences in front of the few clapboard houses already built along a mile-long drive that circled the lake. Wells were bored to tap the underground springs so there would be plenty of drinking water. A wooden sidewalk was built from the post office to the depot on Baldwin Avenue.

30. When the hotels filled, visitors rented tents or built huts on the grounds around Lake DeFuniak. Courtesy of State Archives of Florida.

31. Hotel Chautauqua sprawled along the lake bank at DeFuniak Springs in a wilderness that was mostly known to Scot pioneers and Euchees. Courtesy of State Archives of Florida.

In February, trains pulled into the station carrying visitors from Iowa, Illinois, New York, Minnesota, and South Dakota.[15] The street was packed with crowds from cities and farms.[16] Midwest accents mingled with those of the north and the south. Eventually, up to four thousand passengers arrived by train each day.[17]

The visitors were curious about the exotic Florida wilderness described in promotional literature and pictured on L&N postcards: "The lake in the center of the town, round as the moon and clear as the sky, one mile in circumference and eighty feet in depth is a marvel of beauty," they read in a Hotel Chautauqua pamphlet.[18]

During the day, participants attended various events. Wallace Bruce, who had been the U.S. consul to Scotland in Edinburgh and former editor of the *Yale Literary Magazine,* discussed Robert Burns's work in one room. In another session, Sau Ah Brah, of Burma, talked about the religious and social customs of India. Lydia Von Folkenstein, of Jerusalem, described the Bedouin of Palestine.[19] B. F. Peters, a leading vocal soloist from Indianapolis, coached students on pitch and tone.[20] Music filled the air. Soprano soloists and student choirs performed in the afternoons at an amphitheater that seated twenty-five hundred. Concerts or plays entertained at night.[21]

At this time, Florida was considered exotic in the rest of the country, and visitors likely read guidebooks about the newfound paradise. One was called *Florida Facts, Both Bright and Blue: A Guide Book to Intending Settlers, Tourists, and Investors from a Northerner's Standpoint; Plain Unvarnished Truth, without "Taffy," No Advertisements or Puffs.* This book taught visitors how to eat an orange:

> "Nasty, sloppy things! I won't eat another one this winter!" The speaker was bending with orange juice dripping from each finger, and flecks of yellow sacs bedaubed his mustache and beard. He was a new-comer and had not learned the fine art of orange eating that a Floridian of a month's residence acquires. . . . To enjoy to the full the best of our known fruits, one must needs walk out under the verdant trees, select a medium-sized, thin-skinned russet, pull, pull hard until off it comes, leaving a hole at the stem, "plugged" and worthless for shipping, but just right for eating. Pare it as you would an apple, cut in halves cross ways, and suck from the ruptured cells nectar fit for gods. If more fastidious, use a teaspoon.
>
> Add to the charm of orange eating, a midwinter mid-day, temperature 70 to 80 degrees, rendering open-air exercise a delight, and you have two important reasons why Florida is and always will be popular as a winter resort, especially when it can be reached in thirty-six hours from New York City.[22]

In 1887, just two years after the first session, the Chautauqua was extended to six weeks and added annual meetings of teachers, farmers, and gardeners. A state school to train teachers, the Florida Normal School, was established at DeFuniak Springs.[23] Although the state moved teacher training to Tallahassee several years later, prominent citizens and the Presbyterian Church bought the buildings and founded Palmer College to take its place.[24]

On Circle Drive, rimming the lake, white clapboard houses wrapped by porches trimmed in Victorian gingerbread fretwork were built for the Bruces and other families. Northerners who built winter cottages became neighbors with Scots who had moved to the lake from the nearby Euchee Valley. As the population increased—to eight hundred residents by the early 1890s—so did the cost of land, from sixty cents an acre in 1882, when the Pensacola and Atlantic Railroad laid its tracks, to $15.95 just eight years later.[25]

On the west side of the lake, a few hundred yards from the Tabernacle and meeting hall, a one-room library opened its doors just before Christmas in

32. As many as four thousand visitors a day arrived at the DeFuniak train depot from as far away as Illinois and South Dakota. Courtesy of Special Collections, University of West Florida Library, Pensacola.

1887.[26] Volumes of John Stoddard's lectures on Florence, Norway, Athens, and other foreign lands were neatly stacked on sturdy wooden shelves. A series called *Messages and Papers of the Presidents* joined *Modern Eloquence*, a collection of after-dinner speeches and various addresses. Those volumes and others are now on display at the library.

The books would be lovingly tended for thirty years by Alice Fellows, a Methodist from Syracuse, New York, who moved to DeFuniak Springs with her brother a few years after the library was built. She apparently governed the stacks with a strict hand, in keeping with the Victorian architecture of the small building. "With Miss Fellows in charge of the library there was never any likelihood of any book of a questionable nature finding its place on the shelves and the DeFuniak library was entirely free of that class of undesirable books, which in this day of free and easy literature, find their way into too many libraries open to the public," said the announcement of her death in the town paper when she died in 1926.[27]

By 1894, those attending the Chautauqua could read about festival activities in the *Daily Local*. The paper cost three cents. On March 6 of that year, the lead story on page one praised a concert by the Schubert Quartet. In the paper, the Opera House Store, owned by W. L. Cawthon and Company, advertised groceries, dry goods, notions, shoes, hats, furniture, and stoves. Stubbs' Bakery promoted fine cakes.[28]

Yet despite nationwide publicity and the impressive growth of DeFuniak Springs, some say the Chautauqua was never a great financial success. The first year, costs reached eleven thousand dollars with a return of only four hundred dollars.[29]

The Florida Chautauqua eventually fell victim to the Roaring Twenties, when lifestyles were again dramatically changed by transportation and technology—this time by the automobile, radio, and movies. Other cities had begun holding Chautauquas of their own, which competed with the one in DeFuniak Springs. In the 1920s, the Florida Chautauqua shriveled. The Bruces moved away. The hotels eventually closed. And the trains began hauling mostly freight.[30]

However, the impact of the Chautauqua extended well beyond the borders of DeFuniak Springs. The lectures and concerts that had brought scholars, artists, and students had created an intellectual atmosphere that counterbalanced the harsh labor conditions of the area's turpentine and lumber industries. DeFuniak Springs itself later made a comeback as a picturesque town, and locals now enjoy a Chautauqua that is again being held every year.

The Chautauqua also created a gateway from DeFuniak Springs to the rest of the Emerald Coast. Families like that of Erwin S. Buck from Ohio moved over to Santa Rosa Sound and to other Panhandle areas.

William Herbert Butler had seen a Chautauqua advertisement while farming in South Dakota in the late 1800s and literally loaded his life onto a boxcar—his wife, children, cattle, and plows. Like many others who made the journey to DeFuniak Springs, Butler stayed.[31]

After working as a real estate agent, he bought land at Grayton Beach, where only a half-dozen houses stood near the dunes and where cattle grazed at General William Miller's homestead on Western Lake. Grayton Beach, which has been ranked as one of the top five ecologically in the country in recent years, was such a bargain in the early 1900s that Butler switched the site of a planned resort to the Gulf Coast from higher-priced Phillips Inlet on Choctawhatchee Bay.

33. Beach attire was much different for tourists at the turn of the twentieth century; here, vacationers are venturing to Santa Rosa Island at Pensacola. Courtesy of Special Collections, University of West Florida Library, Pensacola.

The Grayton Beach parcel was exposed to storms and had already failed once as a tourist spot. But the price was only half that of bay land.[32] Butler built a few cottages that he rented in the summer and over the years sold a few lots.

Chautauqua visitors who rode oxcarts to the Gulf shore on day trips from DeFuniak Springs told others how beautiful the beach was, and Grayton eventually became one of the first beachfront communities of the Emerald Coast. The village remains a cluster of cypress cottages nestled under live oaks near a state nature area and the well-known resort town of Seaside.

Other ventures stemmed from the interest created by the Chautauqua, but not all were successful. Some twenty-five miles south of DeFuniak Springs, on the thumb of land between the Gulf and Choctawhatchee Bay, Chicago doctor Charles Cessna built a bayou town he hoped would rival Pensacola as the largest in the Panhandle.

Cessna had cruised the coast and Choctawhatchee Bay on a steamboat in 1909, savoring the balmy Gulf breeze that was a welcome relief from Chicago's icy north wind off Lake Michigan. When he got back to Illinois, he called his brothers, William, Harry, and Albert, and put together an investment group that planned a coastal city complete with streetcars.

The company bought more than two thousand acres, at $1.75 per acre, from J. J. McCaskill, who owned a Freeport timber mill and store. Cessna and his investors hired H. Heinze, a Chicago civil engineer, to design a city called Colony at Santa Rosa. They decided to sell town and country property in a six-hundred-dollar package that included both a ten-acre farm tract and a fifty-foot lot in the city.[33] Financing was available with a third down and 6 percent interest.

Ads ran in the *Chicago Tribune* and newspapers of other midwestern cities promoting the location of the new town near the famed "Chautauqua of the South" at DeFuniak Springs. "Every day of the year may be spent out of doors," one ad proclaimed.[34]

The coastal soil was free of rocks, promotional literature noted. Although this was true, the land was hardly ready to plant. Loggers had cut the forests of longleaf pines, leaving the land studded with stumps six to eighteen inches around, about thirty-five of them to the acre that would have to be pulled up, burned out, or plowed under.

The ads boasted that fields could produce grapes for market three weeks before California vines, pecan groves that could yield $250 per tree, as well as oranges, figs, blueberries, corn, oats, potatoes, cabbage, beets, onions, and pumpkins.[35]

During the next decade, one thousand people moved to Colony at Santa Rosa. Warehouses, a cannery, a general store, a sawmill, and a hotel turned the bayou banks into a thriving town. Schooners and steamers docked to load vegetables, fruit, eggs, and timber that would be shipped to Pensacola and Mobile. The 172-foot *Charles E. Cessna,* with three decks and a ballroom, carried up to one thousand sightseers who paid six dollars for a round-trip excursion from Mobile.[36]

Just when the town seemed to be flourishing, disaster struck. An orange disease called canker gnawed the roots of satusuma trees. Groves that were not destroyed by disease were ordered burned by the state to prevent contamination of other orchards. A storm flooded sugarcane fields with brackish water. Timber companies depleted the pines and moved on to other tracts. Farms and businesses went broke. Settlers booked passage to Mobile on the steamers that had carried their market crops and left Santa Rosa to start over elsewhere. Cessna sold his land to Alfred I. duPont.[37] Wild boar took over this bank of the Choctawhatchee Bay, and in time the area would be called Hogtown Bayou.

The trains, however, had connected the region to the rest of the country. One who took advantage of the transportation network was the farmer Moses Sapp. He fell into a moneymaking business made possible by the railroad.

He had warned his children time and again to stop sneaking into the snake-infested woods near their house north of Crestview to pick "swamp huckle-berries." They paid him little mind. So Sapp dug up thirty of the wild berry bushes, which grew up to fifteen feet tall in Yellow River swampland, and planted them closer to the house so the children could get to them without going into the forest. Two summers later, about 1912, the bushes were loaded with berries, black "rabbit eyes" touched with blue, bigger than the wild ones and tasting better. Neighbors came by, asking to buy a quart or two.

Before long, Sapp set up an assembly line of tables where his family and other workers culled and packed berries in quart boxes. The small plot of thirty bushes expanded as Sapp transplanted more each winter, with orchards eventually covering twenty acres and producing four thousand quarts a year. The cultivated bushes came to be known as blueberries.[38]

The railroad that had opened the pioneer land to trade and settlement took Sapp's berries to northern markets. A route to Chicago linked his or-chard to Frank Goll's MarGol Health Products, which mixed the berries into a tonic.[39]

Sapp advised anyone wanting to make "easy money" to cultivate the swamp huckleberries. His favorite grove yielded fourteen to forty quarts per bush a year, paying about five hundred dollars an acre.[40] Other farmers began grow-ing blueberries, too, and the area came to be called the Blueberry Capital of America.[41]

Though trains spurred businesses such as Sapp's, other areas suffered from the lack of rail transportation. A planned track through St. Andrews in the area near present-day Panama City failed to materialize for years. Without trains, such coastal communities had to rely on water transport.[42]

In 1885, the St. Andrews Bay Railroad Land and Mining Company out of Cincinnati, Ohio, tried to start a town by selling twenty-five by eighty-two-foot lots for $1.25.[43] A one-bedroom home cost three hundred dollars and a two-story house cost fifteen hundred.[44] The venture was one of the first Florida attempts to sell real estate by mail. Ads showed women and children picking oranges and proclaimed the country a lush paradise by the sea. But the development failed because the area was so remote and the railroad was not built. Those who did buy land had to get there by boat because there were few roads. They usually arrived on a schooner, such as the *Nettie,* from Pensacola. Others came from New Orleans aboard the steamship *Cumberland.*[45]

"At St. Andrews Bay, when the vessel hove in sight, the mills began tooting their whistles, every body that could get a horn began blowing his instrument, and the whole population turned out and went down to the wharf to welcome the strangers," said the *Pensacola Commercial.* "As the vessel approached the shore, the people set up a grand hurrah, the mills and horns again began their tooting and the woods resounded with the clamor made in honor of the occasion."[46]

Some who bought land were disappointed and left. Others built log cottages or camped in tents. Park House offered boarding for three dollars a month.[47] Many planted orange groves that could yield up to 225 oranges per tree.[48]

Under the Homestead Act, government land was available to settlers in 160-acre parcels for $1.25 an acre if the buyer agreed to live on the property for fourteen months during five years. But because the coast was so isolated, homesteader Samuel Erwin couldn't even give away land.[49]

However, one man saw potential for the area. George Mortimer West, a railroad executive from Chicago, vacationed at St. Andrews Bay in the late 1800s. His wife suffered from a respiratory illness, and West thought the warmer climate would be healthier for her, so they moved to a community called Harrison—named after President Benjamin Harrison.[50] Only a few families lived there after the Civil War.[51]

West and other investors bought tracts and created the Gulf Coast Development Company to sell stock for property that would be a town. Lots cost $150 to $300 each. West named the town Panama City because it was on a line between Chicago and the Panama Canal, which was then being built. He published a newspaper, the *Panama City Pilot,* and opened a bank. A three-story hotel, the Gulf View Inn, was the largest building in town. A cotton gin, café, and drugstore were built at the city docks.[52]

Panama City was incorporated with several hundred residents. After seventy years of trying to get a railroad, the Atlanta and St. Andrews Bay line finally was completed in 1908. The train provided an alternative to boats and stagecoaches.[53] A resort was built on Massalina Bayou, and businesses dotted the shoreline.[54]

Another developer, Senator W. H. Lynn of New York, visited the Panama City area and bought land at a railroad station on North Bay. He advertised fifty-dollar lots with five farming acres in the *National Tribune* in Washington, D.C., a newspaper popular with Civil War veterans. Many of them bought lots, and the town population grew to five hundred. It was named Lynn Haven.[55]

Before 1908, when ice plants were first built, the leading commercial business in Panama City was salting fish. Miles-long schools of mullet and endless catches of redfish, snapper, and grouper established St. Andrews Bay as a fisherman's dream.[56] Boat operators like Charley Anderson unloaded thousands of pounds of fish at the docks. Crews of twenty men stood at long tables under shed roofs to split and salt the fish. They would stack the fish in wagons or pack it in barrels holding a hundred pounds. People came from miles away by wagon to get salt and to fish.[57]

Meanwhile, as Panama City and Pensacola grew on each side of the Emerald Coast, the Destin area remained a small fishing village. However, the Fort Walton Beach area began attracting tourists, some of them famous.

Places to Visit

Walking tour of historic homes around lake and the old library building, DeFuniak Springs.

Grayton Beach, County Road 30-A, south of U.S. Highway 98, halfway between Panama City and Destin. County Road 283 from U.S. Highway 98. Left on 30-A.

Site of Colony at Santa Rosa at Hogtown Bayou, County Road 395, off U.S. Highway 98, Hogtown Bayou Lane, Santa Rosa.

Books to Read

We Called It Culture: The Story of Chautauqua, by Victoria Case and Robert Ormond Case (Garden City, N.Y.: Doubleday, 1948).

8. Characters, Celebrities—and Outlaws

The narrow channel between Santa Rosa Island and the mainland, less than a quarter mile wide in places, became a water highway in the late 1800s and early 1900s bringing wealthy timber owners and politicians from Pensacola on board the paddleboat *Captain Fritz*. A parade of characters, celebrities—and outlaws—followed over the next fifty years, turning one section of this isolated coast from a last frontier into a little Las Vegas. Area folklore is filled with names of the famous and notorious, including comedian Bob Hope, country music legend Hank Williams, train robber Rube Burrows, and organized-crime king Al Capone.

Guests stayed at the Harbeson Hotel for twenty-one dollars a week and danced to a six-piece band on a pavilion built over the water. They paid twenty-five cents for a boat ride to Pirates Cove, where they heard the story of "the Ghost of Lady's Walk." According to the legend, a pirate had cut off the head of a damsel, and by the light of a full moon she would return, floating amid the dunes, wailing, holding her head in her hands, and sweeping the sand with her hair. Those listening to the story watched apprehensively to see if she would appear.[1]

Ghosts were also reported in the woods that are now part of Tyndall Air Force Base at Panama City. A mysterious light sometimes appeared, floating eerily among the trees. Some said it was merely swamp gas, but others were convinced the light came from ghosts. Runway lights now obscure the mysterious glow.[2]

The land seemed to invite extremes: romance and recklessness; nature's beauty and nightlife's bounty.

At Buck's Store in Camp Walton, there was no telling who would come in the back door that opened onto Santa Rosa Sound. Owner Erwin S. Buck, an Ohio native who had moved from DeFuniak Springs, stocked the store with "everything but babies and coffins," according to *Recollections,* a booklet published by the Junior Service League of Fort Walton Beach.

Before Charles Lindbergh became famous for crossing the Atlantic, he once made an emergency landing on the Emerald Coast when his plane's oil line broke. He went to Buck's Store and purchased repair materials.

Wallis Simpson, the divorcée for whom King Edward VIII would give up the British throne, is said to have stopped by to drink colas on two occasions while yachting with friends.[3] She was living in Pensacola, where she met her first husband.

A character in one of the world's great love stories, Simpson is perhaps the most intriguing symbol of the romantic aura of this exotic region in the 1900s. In April 1916, the young debutante Bessie Wallis Warfield flipped through her stylish skirts, blouses, and frocks, trying to decide which to pack for Florida, where pink azaleas and white oleanders were already in bloom. The nineteen-year-old boarded a train to Jacksonville, then switched to her Uncle Solomon Warfield's railroad that crossed the Panhandle to Pensacola.[4] At the station she was met by her cousin Corinne Barnett Mustin, whose husband, Henry, was commander of America's first navy air base, then being established in Pensacola. It was the year before the United States would enter World War I.[5]

34. Businesses like Buck's Store opened to Santa Rosa Sound at Camp Walton, pictured here. Visitors included Charles Lindbergh and Wallis Simpson. By permission of the Williams Gallery, DeFuniak Springs, Fla.

35. Earl W. Spencer Jr., seated second from left, with officers at Pensacola Naval Aeronautic Station in 1915, just thirteen years after the Wright brothers' first flight. Courtesy of the Naval Historical Foundation.

The naval air station rejuvenated Pensacola's economy, which had lagged when the lumber boom ended and military activity stalled. Before the base was established, two banks had failed and there had even been talk of closing the Pensacola forts altogether, which would have meant that for the first time the city would not be a military post. The naval air base began in 1914 with only nine officers, twenty-three enlisted men, and seven planes, but money poured in for construction projects, and more airmen soon arrived. The naval air station was built on a bluff where Tristán de Luna had failed to establish a colony in the sixteenth century. The site was where the navy yard had been rebuilt after the Civil War, when Confederates had demolished it rather than let it fall into Union hands.

Captain W. I. Chambers of the Navy Department watched with great interest when the first seaplane and aircraft carrier were built in 1911. He was named head of a board to develop naval aviation and picked Pensacola for the country's only flight training center. Within a few years, the station grew to 438 officers and 5,538 enlisted men, most of them graduates of Annapolis. The Pensacola station became known as the "Annapolis of the Air."[6] Construction on the base amounted to four hundred thousand dollars a month and provided numerous jobs.[7]

A housing shortage resulted, and many Pensacola residents provided room and board to the servicemen and other workers. In just twenty years, the population nearly doubled, soaring from 38,606 in 1900 to 63,056 in 1920.[8]

Young ladies of Pensacola welcomed the influx of dashing pilots. Among them was the young debutante Wallis Warfield, who fell in love with the airmen and the exotic town.

At the commandant's house overlooking Pensacola Bay, three young officers joined Wallis and her cousin one afternoon for lunch. That night, in a letter to her mother, Wallis wrote, "I have just met the world's most fascinating aviator." He was Lieutenant Earl Winfield Spencer Jr., nicknamed "Win," from a prominent Chicago family and who was one of the military's first flyers.[9]

"Every generation has its own set of heroes, and mine were the gay, gallant fliers of Pensacola," Wallis wrote in her memoir, *The Heart Has Its Reasons.* She had never seen an airplane before and watched these first boxy ones with fabric wings tilt and dip while trying to lift off over Pensacola Bay.[10] This was only thirteen years after the Wright brothers' first flight.

Those days on the base were a mixture of gaiety and grief. During Wallis's stay, plane crashes killed two young pilots. That threat of death hovering over every day gave an edge to the sleepy mood of the port town. At night, the young fliers and their dates dismissed the dangers of day and whirled through dinners and dances at the San Carlos Hotel.[11] The grand eight-story Spanish-style hotel was built in 1910 and claimed to be one of the most modern in the South.

On outings with Corinne or dates with young officers, Wallis ferried across Pensacola Bay to Santa Rosa Beach for picnics and walks to look for seashells.[12] Afternoon excursions on the bay included cruising down the coast to Camp Walton and stopping at Buck's Store. The heart of the Emerald Coast remained a frontier.

Wallis would have seen Santa Rosa Island as "a wilderness of magnificent live-oaks, magnolias and longleaf yellow pines spreading over white, red and yellow bluffs, to port," as described by F. F. Bingham in his log aboard the *Peep*

36. A flimsy plane takes off from a ship at Naval Air Station Pensacola in 1915. Courtesy of State Archives of Florida.

O' Day in 1912, just a few years before Wallis cruised the waters. "There is over forty miles of the desert island, laying ten to one hundred feet above the sea, its surface taking all the odd and fantastic shapes of wind-blown sand; there are gorges and canyons, plateaus and wide stretches of land that look like a sea's ghost, waves of sand struck dead and white in midair."[13]

Wallis would have passed by the Cedars resort hotel on the sound at Mary Esther.[14] She might have stopped to climb "Hollow Hill," a hundred-foot-high sand dune on Santa Rosa Island. At Camp Walton, later named Fort Walton Beach, she would have seen three hotels and several camps.[15] The Narrows, a strip of water before Santa Rosa Sound merges with Choctawhatchee Bay, was "fairly alive with motor boats of all descriptions," wrote Bingham.[16]

In Pensacola, Wallis was spending more and more time with Win, and she extended her stay from one to two months. One night after a movie, the couple stopped by the country club, walked out onto the porch, and Win asked her to marry him. Like dozens of other young women who fell in love with cadets, she said yes.[17]

On November 8 in Baltimore, by evening candlelight, Wallis slowly walked down the aisle of Christ Episcopal Church in a white velvet gown, carrying a bouquet of orchids and lilies of the valley.[18]

Wallis had not noticed Win's fondness for liquor during their courtship. The first indication she had that there was a problem was on their honeymoon at the Greenbriar in West Virginia, which was a dry state. Win panicked but then remembered he had packed gin for an emergency.[19]

Wallis and Win returned to Pensacola and moved into a three-bedroom white frame cottage, the fifth one from the bay on Admiralty Row. "The view over the bay was lovely, and I was young and wide-eyed in a world that was not only new but brave," she wrote in her memoir. She had the furniture painted white and hired a cook and a maid at thirty-two dollars a month. In the evenings, she and Win joined other couples for dinner followed by bridge or poker. On Saturday nights, they continued their tradition of dancing at the San Carlos. "What we Navy wives really lived for was Saturday night," Wallis wrote. "Then all restrictions were off, and we went to town literally and

37. Spencer's classmate, Lieutenant Commander William M. Corry, on a bare-bones seaplane in 1915. Two pilots died in crashes while Wallis Simpson was visiting in Pensacola. Courtesy of State Archives of Florida.

figuratively. Dressed in our best we descended on the San Carlos Hotel for a night of wining, dining and dancing into the small hours."[20] At dances and parties, Wallis flirted with other men while Win sat in a corner drinking and sulking.[21]

More cadets arrived at the base, which was running in high gear as the military prepared for war. On April 6, 1917, a year after Wallis first came to Pensacola, America entered the war that President Woodrow Wilson said would make the world safe for democracy.

Win was transferred in turn to Boston, San Diego, and then Washington, D.C. Wallis loved the social life with government officials and diplomats in the nation's capital. Win continued drinking heavily. When he got orders to be stationed in Hong Kong, Wallis remained in Washington. She had an affair with an Argentine diplomat but joined Win in China after he begged her to give him another chance. The reunion only lasted two weeks before Win came home drunk.

Wallis moved out and traveled in China, playing poker to supplement her wife's allotment and was escorted to restaurants and parties by eligible young men. She returned to Washington and finally, in 1927, got a divorce. A year later, Wallis married Ernest Simpson, whom she had met in New York, and they moved to London, where he owned a ship brokerage. A social climber, Wallis was thrilled when they began getting invitations from British high society.[22]

There are several versions of how she met Prince Edward of Wales, the future king of England, but at some point Wallis and Ernest were invited to the prince's country house. It was the beginning of a relationship that would make headlines around the world. The three dined together in the best restaurants and became immensely popular with the top ranks of high society. Edward often stopped by the Simpsons' house, sometimes when Ernest was not at home. The prince and Wallis began spending more and more time alone together.[23]

Edward invited the Simpsons to go with him on a trip to Europe in August 1934. Ernest had to decline because of business matters, so Wallis went alone. On an eleven-day cruise together along the Spanish and Portuguese coasts, Wallis realized their relationship had crossed over from friendship to love. Wallis assumed the role of hostess at Edward's estate, giving orders to servants and planning social events.[24]

Her prince charming became king in 1936 when his father, George V, died. As Edward was pronounced king, Wallis stood by his side.[25] She later discovered that Ernest was having a love affair with an old friend from America, and she filed for divorce. Meanwhile, King Edward began referring to her as his future wife. Legally, the king could marry a divorced woman, though it would cause an uproar in the church, royal family, Parliament, and cabinet, since divorce was not yet widely accepted. News of an upcoming marriage that would coincide with the king's coronation appeared in an American newspaper, but the story did not run in England. When the British press later published the story, the country was shocked.[26]

The king began to think of abdicating. Some advisors urged him to consider marriage with the stipulation that Wallis would remain a commoner. However, that alternative would require legislation that was unlikely to pass. Others urged him to delay marriage. To avoid publicity, Wallis fled to France to stay with friends. Edward decided to give up the throne after serving as king for 325 days. He told his country in a famous radio address that he was abdicating to marry the woman he loved. He was given the title Duke of Windsor and went to Vienna to wait a few months for Wallis's divorce to be final.[27]

They married in a French chateau, and Wallis became the Duchess of Windsor. It had been twenty years since she had met her first love on the Panhandle coast. After a honeymoon touring Europe and America, the royal couple lived in France and later the Bahamas, spending their years wandering the world.[28]

At the time when Wallis first visited Pensacola, a fourth of Florida's residents lived in the Panhandle. The war spurred shipbuilding as well as aviation training at Pensacola, with fifteen hundred workers employed by the Pensacola Shipbuilding Company. More people moved into the city. The population soared by ten thousand in just two years.[29] Growth in the region, however, was concentrated in Pensacola and inland towns. As Destin fisherman Joseph Marler was fond of saying, the coast itself was only good for fleas and children.[30]

During Prohibition, the remote waterways and sparsely populated wilderness of the Panhandle became tempting channels for rumrunners. A boat loaded with whiskey ran aground off East Pass and had to dump the cargo overboard. Local fisherman Captain Homer Jones said that he and his crew

38. The Duchess and Duke of Windsor at the Horseshoe Plantation near Tallahassee in 1947. Their romance was made famous by Prince Edward's abdication of the British throne so he could marry the twice-divorced Wallis. Courtesy of State Archives of Florida.

saw burlap sacks filled with half pints in the clear water. They dove in and pulled up fifteen cases of liquor.[31]

Some boat owners made extra cash during Prohibition by hauling whiskey from rumrunners to inland sites. One mission ran afoul when the captain of a rumrunner failed to get an all-clear signal and reluctantly decided to dump the whiskey. Jones said he heard of the incident and searched the seas. He found ten wooden boxes filled with quart bottles of whiskey and gin.[32] Another rumrunner, the *Glendoveer,* sank near Beacon Beach at Panama City. When it was hauled up, the boat was loaded with whiskey and wine.[33]

Like most areas of the country, the Emerald Coast had its share of bootleggers. Selling liquor was one of the few ways to make money in some communities, locals recall. Hard times followed the nationwide economic collapse after the stock market crashed in 1929. Nationally, enforcement authorities grumbled that trying to eliminate bootlegging was a losing battle, with Prohibition getting little public support. In Pensacola, booze lovers took meals to a well-known bootlegger while he was jailed so he would stay healthy.[34]

"The moonshiners used to be from one end of the [Choctawhatchee] river to the other and they used to have to wear badges so they wouldn't sell the moonshine to one another," said Johnnie Morrison, a deputy sheriff in Holmes County, in an oral history by the Northwest Florida Water Management District. Whiskey sold for two dollars a gallon. W. A. White of Point Washington told the oral history interviewer that he made moonshine with white flour instead of corn and bought ten-pound bags of sugar for the mix from several different stores so he wouldn't look suspicious: "it was a way to survive, to buy clothes to wear, and to get something to eat," he explained.[35]

America's most notorious gangster, Al Capone, is said to have visited the Emerald Coast in the early 1930s and to have been behind a rum-running operation with boats loaded with whiskey slipping through East Pass at night during Prohibition. His presence in Florida at the time was well publicized. The gangster who ruled Chicago racketeering lived in a secluded villa surrounded by a concrete wall on Palm Island off Miami Beach.[36]

Local resident Agnes Hall recalled that Capone and his men rented the second floor of the Florosa Inn in the early 1930s when she was manager of the hotel. At the time, she didn't recognize Capone but cautioned him that she would have no drinking or carousing at the inn. A waiter overheard the men talking and learned that the leader was Capone.[37]

Highway construction in the 1920s and 1930s across the Emerald Coast transformed transportation from Pensacola to Panama City. Concrete bridges replaced wooden ones.[38] The Pensacola Bay Bridge was completed, as were three bridges across parts of St. Andrews Bay, so that tourists could more easily get to the beach. Vacationers rented cottages by the sea and flocked to an amusement park. The Destin Bridge was also completed, making that area more accessible. Just as important, the Gulf Coast Highway, now U.S. Highway 98, was built connecting the communities of the Emerald Coast to the east and west.[39]

Interestingly, as roads were built, a rift developed between townspeople and cattle owners whose herds roamed free. The livestock posed a hazard to drivers, but fencing cattle would mean ranchers would have the added expense of feeding their herds. The issue was resolved in 1949 when a law was passed requiring ranchers to fence their animals.[40]

The development of more military posts boosted the economy of the Emerald Coast from one end to the other. The naval air station in Pensacola was expanded, Tyndall Air Force Base was built at Panama City, and Eglin Air Force Base was established at Valparaiso. The military money helped offset the loss of tourist dollars during the Depression and World War II.

Some of the greatest heroes of World War II had flown practice runs at Eglin, and Hollywood cameras rolled when Gregory Peck arrived in Crestview in 1949 to film *Twelve O'Clock High*.[41] Peck donned the uniform and the character of a bomb squadron commander flying missions from England. The movie, which landed the thirty-three-year-old Peck an Oscar nomination for Best Actor, captured the dramatic role of the fliers, many from Eglin Field, who helped win the war in the skies over Europe.

Eglin, which began as a small field in 1934, became a staging ground for one of the most crucial missions of the war. In March 1942, a lieutenant colonel, James H. Doolittle, and his men, called the Raiders, practiced taking off from short runways, getting ready for their biggest assignment: to launch an attack against Tokyo from the decks of the aircraft carrier *Hornet*.[42]

While flyers trained in coastal skies, rumors circulated that German submarines prowled offshore in Gulf waters. At night, residents turned off their car lights when driving along the beach on U.S. Highway 98. Don Adams

39. As much of Florida became developed, the Emerald Coast remained isolated. Even as late as 1950, the shore was desolate. Courtesy of State Archives of Florida.

of Birmingham recalled that when he was a young boy vacationing at Fort Walton Beach, he overheard adults talking about German submarines. He heard rumors that a German lifeboat and parachute had been found on shore. Fears of German submarines in the Gulf were not entirely unfounded. German subs sank three ships in Florida waters in 1942 off the coasts of Jacksonville and Cape Canaveral and German U-boats sank more than twenty-four boats in Florida waters, one of them near Apalachicola.[43]

Soldiers and scientists at Eglin Air Force Base tested combat equipment as well as aircraft. In 1944, when the Germans attacked England with V-1 and V-2 rockets, Eglin built mock bunkers and launch ramps, as well as missiles, to simulate enemy facilities and test ways of destroying them. As the Allies fought Germany and Japan, the base grew into a major command center. The McKinley Climatic Laboratory created conditions of desert and arctic terrain to test extreme temperatures on equipment and soldiers. The base now has areas that look like a *Star Wars* set, where tests are conducted in electronic combat using cluster munitions and sensor-fused weapons.[44]

Now covering much of two counties, Walton and Okaloosa, Eglin originated as a small airport for pilots who flew to the coast to play golf when on leave from Maxwell Field in Montgomery. The pilots at first landed on the golf fairways of a Valparaiso resort. The hangar and land were donated to the military in the mid-1930s for what was first called Valparaiso Bombing and Gunnery Base. The field was renamed in honor of a popular Maxwell pilot, Frederick I. Eglin, who was killed in a crash near Anniston, Alabama, in 1937. The Choctawhatchee National Forest was transferred to the base in 1940, significantly expanding Eglin and providing more acreage for military maneuvers.[45] Spin-off businesses to support the base boosted Fort Walton Beach. Eglin brought soldiers with steady paychecks—and a yen for off-hours fun.

The Pensacola Naval Air Station was expanded on the eve of World War II to train eleven hundred cadets a month, again ensuring the port's significance as a military base.[46] During the war, twenty-seven thousand airmen trained at the air station. The city's population jumped to seventy-seven thousand in 1945 from fifty-eight thousand in 1940.[47]

The cadets from Pensacola were among the first to hear a young country singer who got his first break from a musician, Neal "Pappy" McCormick, from DeFuniak Springs in the heart of the Emerald Coast. McCormick played guitar and sang at nightspots along the Panhandle, as well as on the Pensacola radio station WCOA. During one of the broadcasts in the late 1930s, at studios on the top floor of the San Carlos Hotel, a skinny teenager named Hank Williams waited with his band to audition.

McCormick thought the boy from Montgomery sounded pretty good and invited him to play a dance gig with his Barn Dance Troubadours that night at the Hippodrome skating rink on West Cervantes. Williams put his soul into his voice, and the crowd loved him. McCormick hired him at eight dollars a week, plus meals and travel expenses, and gradually took on the other three members of Williams's band.[48]

For several years, Williams sang with the Troubadours at honky-tonks in Panhandle towns. At Panama City they would ride to the beach in a white limousine, and on one trip to the coastal town Williams wrote "Praying for the Day When Peace Will Come."[49] His voice blended with an electric guitar contraption McCormick had invented using a railroad tie, barbecue spit, and four guitar necks.[50]

Gambling was a favorite pastime at Fort Walton Beach. In the 1940s at Club Shalimar, near Garnier Bayou, gilt chandeliers cast a soft light in the dining room. A band played the tango and other favorites while waiters served gourmet dinners and cocktails. Gamblers tried their luck in an adjoining plush-carpeted room filled with tables for roulette, dice, and blackjack. Gambling was not illegal in Florida at that time. Other gambling spots lined downtown streets, mostly small clubs and bars. Slot machines were everywhere—in hotels, drugstores, and all up and down the streets. Parents even gave their children change to play the gambling machines.[51]

Locals recall that Bob Hope, Vaughn Monroe, and other famous people performed in area supper clubs. Families celebrated anniversaries and birthdays at the clubs, sometimes driving for miles for the good food and entertainment.[52] The area's popular nightlife dimmed, however, on May 31, 1949, when the *Tampa Tribune* kicked off a series about gambling by focusing on Fort Walton as Florida's Las Vegas, where "casino gambling is so wide open you can hear the chips rattle from the main street."

Pressure to stop gambling throughout the state mounted. The *Miami Herald* and the Miami Crime Commission called for reform. Florida was pushed into the national limelight when the U.S. Senate's Kefauver Committee investigated organized crime and held hearings in Miami.[53] Governor Fuller

40. International Paper Company's pulp mill in Panama City employed six hundred workers. Courtesy of State Archives of Florida.

Warren, criticized for allowing casinos to operate, eventually suspended several Panhandle law enforcement officers and others around the state.[54] The far-reaching influence of the Kefauver Committee ended Florida's high profile gambling, shutting down Fort Walton's blackjack and roulette game rooms.

Meanwhile, Eglin continued to expand, becoming one of the largest military bases in the world, with 800 buildings and 724 square miles of land, 4,000 officers, and 10,000 soldiers.[55] Military bases also boosted the economy of the east and west sides of the Emerald Coast and helped those towns recover from the Depression. In Pensacola, the navy complex is still important to the economy, providing jobs for sixteen thousand military personnel and seventy-four hundred civilians.[56]

On the eve of World War II, the ten-million-dollar Tyndall Air Field was built at St. Andrews Bay on twenty-eight thousand acres, most of which Alfred I. duPont owned. The actor Clark Gable was one of the nearly three thousand airmen who trained at the Air Corps gunnery school.[57] In 1945, a navy base, the Coastal Systems Station, was moved to Panama City from Solomons, Maryland, to research and test amphibious warfare.[58]

Pulp and paper and nylon fibers industries brought more civilian jobs, helping to offset the loss of sawmills. International Paper Company built a mill at Bay Harbour in Panama City that employed six hundred workers. They fed logs into chippers and then into vats, which created pulp that was then made into huge rolls of paper. Boatbuilding also provided jobs in communities around St. Andrews Bay. At Carter Craft Corporation, more than seventeen hundred boats were built a year.[59]

In the 1960s and 1970s tourism increased. The wilderness and water of the middle of the Emerald Coast attracted increasing numbers of fishermen, hunters, and nature lovers. Empty stretches of sand and scrub gave way to motels and summer cottages.

The secluded shore that had been a last frontier of Florida became a region with a national reputation for white beaches and emerald water. One of the first modern resorts in the Destin area was Sandestin, a sprawling complex

41. More than seventeen hundred boats a year were being built at Carter Craft Boats in Panama City in 1960. Courtesy of State Archives of Florida.

42. In 1955, Destin Fishing Rodeo drew anglers to the remote coast, little known to tourists. Courtesy of State Archives of Florida.

43. Boats docking at Destin harbor in 1974, when the heart of the Emerald Coast was beginning to be discovered by tourists. Courtesy of State Archives of Florida.

44. The fishing fleet at Destin marina grew in 1977. In 2006, more than one hundred charter boats docked in the harbor to take fishermen to deep water close to shore. Courtesy of State Archives of Florida.

45. An amusement park drew tourists to the more developed Panama City in 1979. The motels and nightlife there were a sharp contrast to Destin. Courtesy of State Archives of Florida.

on twenty-four hundred acres on the beach and bay that opened in 1973. Part of the complex declared bankruptcy in 1990 but has since recovered and expanded. The resort includes four golf courses, tennis courts, a marina, and a village of shops and restaurants.[60] Other development projects spread along the coast of Destin with condos replacing cottages. Now the Emerald Coast is one of the most popular vacation destinations in Florida, and much of the landscape has changed dramatically from solitary stretches of sand to a skyline of towering condominiums. Parts of U.S. Highway 98 that used to be a sand trail are now eight-lane expressways to accommodate the crowds.

In contrast, Seaside was built as a quaint village that has attracted international attention. The project began in 1981 after Robert Davis of Birmingham inherited eighty acres of Gulf front property from his grandfather, who had bought the land in 1946.

Miami architects Andres Duany and Elizabeth Plater-Zyberk developed a master plan with advice from renowned British architect Leon Krier. Victorian cottages in pastel colors with porches and picket fences line narrow streets. The design encourages walkers to enjoy a commons area along with shops and restaurants. "The beaches of South Walton County were part of what some people derisively called the Redneck Riviera. But Seaside turned that image on its head," wrote Kathryn Ziewitz and June Wiaz in *Green Empire: The St. Joe Company and the Remaking of Florida's Panhandle.*[61]

Seaside has been featured in national magazines such as *Architectural Digest* and prominent newspapers including the *New York Times.* The so-called New Urban town even caught the fancy of royalty. Soon after Seaside was developed in the early 1980s, Prince Charles and Princess Diana visited; afterward, the heir to the British crown, long interested in urban planning and architecture, praised Seaside in his book *A Vision of Britain* and on a BBC program.[62] He commissioned Krier as a consultant in building four Dorset villages modeled on the Emerald Coast town.

Lance Armstrong, the seven-time winner of the Tour de France, vacationed at nearby Grayton Beach with Sheryl Crow after one of his victories.[63] He received frowns from Seaside residents when he rode his bike on the pavement instead of on a bike path.[64] Other beachside communities have copied the famed Seaside and have also attracted notable figures. Karl Rove, the powerful advisor to President George W. Bush, owns a house in Rosemary Beach.[65]

46. Prince Charles of England and Princess Diana visited Seaside in the early 1980s and praised the quaint town for its urban planning and design. Courtesy of State Archives of Florida.

More construction is on the way. One reason much of the region remained undeveloped for so many years is because St. Joe Paper Company owned vast tracts that it replanted for forests to supply its pulp and paper machines. St. Joe, which was owned by Alfred I. duPont and Mead Company of Ohio, controlled the way the Panhandle looked for decades. DuPont and his wife, Jessie, moved to Jacksonville in 1926 and began investing in northwest Florida land. The family had made its fortune producing gunpowder and, later, chemicals.[66]

DuPont's brother-in-law, Edward Ball, bounced over sand roads in a Chevy in the 1920s and 1930s and bought thousands of acres at a time for the duPonts. The duPonts bought twelve miles of shoreline property in Walton County for eleven dollars an acre in 1925. The St. Joe Company became the largest private landowner in Florida, making it a powerful economic and political force. The company owned nine hundred thousand acres of Panhandle property. DuPont and Ball were instrumental in getting highways and bridges built across the region.[67]

St. Joe created a real estate company to develop much of its vast holdings. Beachfront resorts built along the former back road of County Road 30-A near Seaside include The Retreat and Watercolor. One tract, sold by St.

Joe to developers who later went bankrupt, is now a state-owned preserve. The Nature Conservancy bought the prized land in a courthouse auction and then sold it to the state, which established Topsail Hill State Preserve and Point Washington State Forest.[68]

Development of the coast is drastically changing the landscape, making the natural areas all the more prized for showcasing the features that make the Emerald Coast special.

These natural features have played a crucial role in the history of this shore for twelve thousand years. Ancient tribes depended on the Gulf, bay, and rivers for food. Sam Story and the Scots relied on waterways for transportation and on forests for game. The bounty of the sea enabled Leonard Destin to found a fishing village. During the Civil War, the Gulf supplied prized salt. Sawmill owners like William Henry Weslie profited from vast timber stands, which also yielded gum for turpentine. Modern charter boat owners take advantage of deep water close to shore.

The Emerald Coast environment that draws increasing numbers of visitors is unique, featuring clear, green Gulf water, thirty-foot dunes, rare coastal lakes, groves of cypress, and miles of marshes. But the Emerald Coast faces challenges in protecting those features; the first step to meeting these challenges is to understand the rare ecology that makes the shore special.

Places to Visit

Air Force Armament Museum, Eglin Air Force Base, Eglin Parkway (Florida 85), north of Fort Walton Beach.

National Museum of Naval Aviation, U.S. Naval Air Station, Building 3465, Pensacola.

Books to Read

Our Town (Fort Walton Beach, Fla.: Northwest Florida Daily News, 1992).

Green Empire: The St. Joe Company and the Remaking of Florida's Panhandle, by Kathryn Ziewitz and June Wiaz (Gainesville: University Press of Florida, 2005).

Florida's Northwest: First Places, Wild Places, Favorite Places, by Michael O'Donovan; photographs by Robin Rowan (Pensacola: Terra Nova Publishing, 2005).

Florida's Miracle Strip: From Redneck Riviera to Emerald Coast, by Tim Hollis (Jackson: University Press of Mississippi, 2004).

The Bay Country of Northwest Florida, by Marlene Womack (Apalachicola, Fla.: New Hope Press, 1998).

Pensacola: Spaniards to Space-Age, by Virginia Parks (Pensacola: Pensacola Historical Society, 1986).

Seaside, by Steven Brooke (Gretna, La.: Pelican Publishing Company, 1995).

9. World beneath the Waves

More than a hundred charter boats, the largest fleet in Florida, dock at Destin harbor—a point of pride with the Emerald Coast Convention and Visitors Bureau. Anglers from all over the world come here, where Gulf depths drop to a hundred feet within ten miles of shore, putting deep-blue fishing within short range.

The deep water is the beginning of a dramatic undersea depression that culminates in a canyon more than three thousand feet deep that slices into the Gulf floor. The submerged, S-shaped ravine called DeSoto Canyon is more than half as deep as the Grand Canyon. The enormous formation measures 137 by 60 miles.

DeSoto Canyon "is one of the largest and most significant structures in the Gulf," according to Jack Reed, a retired geologist who spent forty years studying Gulf formations.[1] This remarkable natural feature brings deep blue water closer to shore at Destin than anywhere else along the Gulf Coast. Fishermen departing from the coast quickly reach seemingly bottomless cobalt waters where eight-foot marlin, nine-hundred-pound blue marlin, and hundred-pound sailfish swim. The bountiful catch from these waters for generations has earned Destin the title "The World's Luckiest Fishing Village."[2]

The giant gorge remained a mystery for centuries. Through the ages explorers sailed over DeSoto Canyon, but the contours of the canyon and life that might live there would not be known for hundreds of years. One of the first references to DeSoto Canyon was recorded in 1878 at a meeting of the American Association for the Advancement of Science. Caleb G. Forshey of New Orleans described an "enormous" depression that extended from a valley in the central Gulf toward Pensacola and Mobile bays. He made his discovery by dropping a weighted line from his boat every twenty miles.[3] The process was slow, tedious, and often inaccurate. Taking those soundings revealed little about what the Gulf floor looked like or what forms of life, if any, lived there. It has been said that when twentieth-century scientists began exploring outer space, they knew more about the near side of the moon than the bottom of our own oceans.[4]

Eventually, high-tech equipment was invented to solve the mysteries of the deep. Sonar, video cameras, and robots developed for the navy in the 1960s revealed more about the undersea landscape, as well as ocean plant and animal life.[5] So did explorations of the Gulf floor by corporations looking for valuable oil deposits. A team of sixteen scientists explored the depths of the canyon in 2004 as part of Deep Scope, a project by the Harbor Branch Oceanographic Institute of Fort Pierce, Florida, and funded by the National Oceanic and Atmospheric Administration. Their research vessel was equipped with a minisubmarine that probed beneath the surface. An underwater camera system photographed deep-sea creatures.[6]

On a map, the Gulf of Mexico is shaped like a fat face, spreading eleven hundred miles from one ear to the other and eight hundred miles from forehead to chin. Nearly encircled by land, five U.S. states form a cap along its northern rim while Mexico curls around the left cheek and under the jaw. To the right of a lopsided grin, where Cuba protrudes like a fine cigar, the Gulf opens to the exotic Caribbean—a link that comes as no surprise to those who see a similarity in the Emerald Coast's clear, green water. Together they form the American Mediterranean, a neck of the Atlantic crossed by the string of Caribbean island pearls.

The Gulf floor is a craggy terrain of plateaus, cliffs, plains, trenches, ridges, and reefs. A shelf 8–135 miles wide circles the Gulf, creating a rim around the basin where the continent slips into the sea.[7] The dramatic depression of DeSoto Canyon cuts through the shelf, splitting the Gulf into two very different east and west sides. The difference between the two sides is remarkable. They have in common an overall subfloor of hardened basalt spewed by volcanoes half a billion years ago.[8] West of the Canyon, a seabed of riverborne sediments, ten miles thick in some places, covers the basalt. Salt domes form a series of hills and ridges sometimes ten thousand feet thick. At New Orleans, the Mississippi River fans out into the Gulf, leaving layers of mud.[9]

In contrast, east of DeSoto Canyon, a quirk of nature along the Emerald Coast produces the clear green water for which the beach is acclaimed. No rivers empty directly into the sea here, though more than 150 rivers feed the rest of the Gulf.[10] Unlike the western section of the Gulf, the sediment-free water along the Emerald Coast remains clear, with an underwater visibility of

47. Its clear blue water and sugar white sand earned Grayton Beach a designation as one of the best in the world. Photo by Jean Lufkin Bouler.

thirty to eighty feet.[11] The crystal clear water enables divers to see fascinating formations. Natural reefs develop layers that form limestone ledges. Covered by sea sponges and sea fans, the reefs hide amberjack, snapper, and grouper.

Almost every part of the Gulf offers special marine life. Underwater meadows of sea grass form a miles-long band on the continental shelf in up to thirty feet of water. These beds of dark green grass indirectly nourish as many as four hundred species of sea creatures, such as worms, snails, sand dollars, shrimp, crabs, and loggerhead turtles, as well as many types of fish.[12]

In these waters just offshore, pompano, often called Florida's most popular food fish, scoot through shallows to find sand fleas and mole shrimp. Schools of cigar minnows feeding on plankton attract streamlined, twenty-pound king mackerel. In the spring, long cobias that can weigh thirty pounds chase migrating manta rays. Tarpon, nearly twice as big as cobias and aptly nicknamed "silver kings," can be heard in a calm sea gulping air when they periodically surface. Female tarpon take thirteen years to mature and spawn, but when they do they release some twelve million eggs.[13]

The continental slope dips deeper and deeper until DeSoto Canyon creases the sea floor, ending at Sigsbee Plain, where the Gulf floor becomes as flat as a pancake near its center, creating one of the world's most level stretches of ocean floor. Tabasco Knolls and Mexican Ridge are among the formations that ripple its edges.[14]

Discovering what lives in these depths three thousand feet below the surface has been difficult. Scientists studying the hidden underwater world of the Gulf are faced with the same problems plaguing oceanographers trying to probe other deep seas. Corrosion, high water pressure, and darkness hinder even modern tools, writes William J. Broad in *The Universe Below: Discovering the Secrets of the Deep Sea.*

Scientists once thought no life could exist in the dark depths of seas, believing that all ecosystems required photosynthesis, driven by sunlight. But in this untamed frontier, marine life survives by possessing extraordinary characteristics. Many organisms give off light themselves. The angler fish prowls deep Gulf waters, whipping long tentacles that glow in the dark, like a fly fisherman casting his line, to attract and snare prey. Others shine their lights on targets and snatch them with sharp needle-like teeth.[15]

Various fish and other marine organisms live at different depths, adjusting to layers of varying light and pressure. In the bottom layer, some animals,

48. The Destin coast is striking because white sand and green water make the landscape unique. No rivers empty their silt into the Gulf here. Photo by Nicholas Bouler.

such as nearly transparent jellyfish, are essentially made of liquid themselves, which allows them to exist in the environment of extremely high water pressure. Sand dollars snuggle just under the sandy bottom, using tiny tubes to move as well as to eat and breathe. Sea lilies look like flowers gently waving on stems in a breeze but are actually animals and date back to the age of dinosaurs.[16]

Sunlight that does filter into the depths of the Gulf gives the water its rich blue hue. The approximately 2 percent of sunlight that penetrates the sea is scattered by particles and molecules. The effect, called underlight, colors the deep Gulf cobalt blue.[17]

The bottom of the Gulf teems with thousands of species of invertebrates, including shellfish and worms, corals and sponges. Some are especially eye-catching, such as the five-sided starfish, which dates back four hundred million years. Others are extremely dangerous, like the sea wasp, a kind of jellyfish whose sting can kill a man in four minutes.

There are also hundreds of species of vertebrates, including more than eight hundred species of fish alone. Most, such as snapper, mullet, and grouper, live near the bottom or on reefs. Others, like billfish, cobia, and mackerel, live in the middle layer of water. Deep-water fish have amazing features that enable them to withstand tremendous water pressure. Many have sacs called swim bladders that fill with gas to adjust to the pressure. Otherwise, the fish would be crushed to death.[18]

In contrast, dolphins live near the surface of the water, even though they can dive and stay under for six minutes. About nine feet long, dolphins frequently put on a show by surfacing and seeming to somersault through the water. Their cavorting perhaps gives them practice for catching a favorite meal of flying fish. Swimming at up to ten miles per hour, coastal dolphins quickly move across the horizon while beachgoers watch. They have earned a reputation for being intelligent, carrying messages underwater for the navy, and helping injured dolphins by holding them above water.[19]

Surprisingly, the very surface of the Gulf also supports marine life. Microscopic plants and animals called plankton float in clumps in the open waters. Like an oasis in the desert, they are crucial elements in the food chain of the Gulf. Sometimes called weedlines, concentrations of plankton on the water surface are home to snails, crabs, shrimp, frogfish, and sea horses that feed dolphins, cobia, sea turtles, and a host of other sea creatures. Some types of plankton are toxic and can cause problems when their populations explode as "red tides," which can kill fish and cause respiratory problems in humans.[20]

Only a small fraction of the Gulf's layers have been studied. The middle one may contain the most mysteries because it is the most difficult from which to get samples of life to study.

Exactly how the crater of the Gulf basin was created is not known. But scientists know that the configuration of land and water has changed numerous times during the past five hundred million years, with continents drifting apart then crashing together and seas rising and falling with temperatures soaring before plunging.

This part of the planet once looked drastically different. Half a billion years ago, the Gulf might have been part of a landmass that, at some point, collapsed and filled with water. Or it might have been a shallow sea that was gradually pushed deeper by the weight of river sediments and movement from continental drift and shifting seafloors.[21] Millions of years ago, North America might have just been wisps of land with the Gulf, shaped in a triangle, connected to a huge ocean covering most of the top half of the globe. And seventy-five million years ago, according to some theories, the Gulf would have extended all the way to Canada.[22]

However and whenever the Gulf formed, the water filling it originally came from the Atlantic. Today, a vast circulation system accounts for currents in the Gulf. A sixty-mile-wide river from the South Atlantic and Caribbean flows westward through the Yucatan Channel between Mexico and Cuba into the Gulf. The current splits through the Yucatan Channel. Some meanders toward Texas. Much of it veers sharply east to return to the Atlantic through the Straits of Florida, between Key West and Cuba, becoming the Gulf Stream that pushes up the eastern seaboard and across the Atlantic.[23]

The salty seawater that stings our eyes comes from rivers carrying trace amounts of salt, which, over millions of years, has built up in the Gulf. The salinity of the water varies from one area of the Gulf to another, depending on depth. In the deep center, the salinity averages about thirty-six parts per thousand, similar to that of the North Atlantic. At the extremes, there are pockets of super-salty water that have at least two hundred parts per thousand, while freshwater springs on the continental slope have none.[24]

The temperature of surface water in the Gulf ranges from sixty-five degrees in winter to eighty-four degrees in summer. In DeSoto Canyon, it dips below forty degrees.[25]

The Gulf of Mexico is a "cradle of life" for plants and animals, and it is also a roadway of civilization for man. It provides 70 percent of the shrimp caught in this country.[26] Almost 40 percent of commercial fish in the United States are caught in the Gulf.[27] Nearly half of America's import/export freight is transported on the basin.[28]

Meanwhile, along the shore, another natural network exists that is radically different from the undersea landscape deep beneath the waves—a rich borderland where land meets the sea.

Places to Visit

Gulfarium, 1010 Miracle Strip Parkway, Fort Walton Beach.

Books to Read

The Universe Below: Discovering the Secrets of the Deep Sea, by William J. Broad (New York: Simon and Schuster, 1997).

The Gulf of Mexico, Robert H. Gore (Sarasota, Fla.: Pineapple Press, 1992).

Environmental Quality in the Gulf of Mexico: A Citizen's Guide, by Michael Weber, Richard T. Townsend, and Rose Bierce (Washington, D.C.: Center for Marine Conservation, 1992).

10. Sandy Shore

Pam Murfey drove her tan truck across a small bridge where Western Lake narrows to a ribbon before disappearing between twenty-foot dunes at Grayton Beach. On the seat beside the Florida park ranger was a copy of *Florida Wildflowers,* which she referred to often as we explored this preserved natural area of 2,228 acres.

Sandwiched between real estate developments off County Road 30-A, Grayton Beach State Park offers a close-up view of undisturbed shore. Gold and pink lantana and scores of yellow wildflowers reflect the colors of sunset around Western Lake. Black needle rush and other plants and marsh grasses soften its rim, while sunlight glitters on the water like sprinkled diamonds. A stand of slash pines to the east buffers the natural area in deep greens and dark browns from neighboring Seaside. To the west, a slender bird totters on skinny legs in a channel that meanders around sandbars and a marsh.

White dunes topped with swaying sea oats hide the magnificent beach beyond. Guarding the beach like sentries, the dunes are among the tallest in Florida. They began when small mounds of sand were trapped by bits of shells, seaweed, driftwood, and other debris washed ashore. Over time, each little pile slowly became taller and wider as the wind brought more sand and piled it on.[1] The white mounds gradually inched inland as sand on the top spilled down the landward slope.[2]

These fragile sand piles might be expected to disintegrate with the first stiff breeze. Gulf winds pack enough power to destroy much heartier structures, Murfey noted, pointing to a pine trunk that had been split by a gale. But the tenacious roots of sea oats anchor the packed sands. Clumps of sea oats, which resemble tall, tan oat, send out rootlike, subterranean plant stems called rhizomes that spread horizontally and are covered by sand. These rhizomes give rise to stalks that can grow up to six feet tall. The roots eventually reach to a depth of three feet. With the sand now stabilized, other plants can begin to grow.

49. Dunes that look like mounds of sugar protect the shore. Hurricanes in 2005 eroded many of them, emphasizing the fragility of the dune ecosystem. By permission of the Williams Gallery, DeFuniak Springs, Fla.

Many of these plants protect themselves by sprouting thorns. Prickly pear cactus grows in flat oval pads that look like green pancakes turned on edge. Sharp brown thorns and bright yellow blooms adorn the pads. Another plant, called "tread softly" or stinging nettle, grows in tufts and bears little white flowers that camouflage its leaves that are covered with fine, hairlike stingers.

The sand is also decorated with harmless flowers that we might expect to find in tended gardens. Long vines of white and purple morning glories crisscross the dunes. A sister variety, moonvine, blooms in the moonlight. Yellow asters and lavender butterfly peas scatter their bright colors across the sand.

These plants have adapted to salty sea spray and the near-desert conditions of scorching heat and shifting sand. Despite the plants' ability to endure such harsh natural conditions, the plant community is fragile when tampered with by humans. When sea oats are picked, dunes loose their "glue." Without dunes, the land loses its shield from high seas and strong winds, and then the beach loses its reservoir of sand to replenish what is sometimes blown seaward.[3]

The vegetation on the dunes provides habitats for a host of animals, some of them rare. The endangered Choctawhatchee beach mouse scurries amidst the scrub. This light-colored little mammal burrows into the sand; if a snake enters its nest, it quickly digs an escape tunnel and gouges a hole to the surface.[4] The mouse feeds on the seeds and berries of sea oats, yaupon hollies, and other dune plants as well as small insects such as beetles. It limits its activity to nighttime, when darkness offers cover from owls, cats, herons, and other predators.[5] But this little animal has no protection from real estate development, which in many areas has destroyed its coastal scrub habitat.

On one of the Grayton Beach dunes, a weathered cedar pavilion perches on pole legs. By climbing several steps to a deck on the Gulf side, visitors are treated to an uncluttered view of a beach acclaimed in national magazines and newspapers. The splendid panorama calls to mind Virginia Woolf's reflective words "Pure sea water on pure sand is almost the loveliest thing in the world."[6]

A white, sandy band borders the brilliant turquoise and emerald hues of the Gulf. The scene looks like a watercolor painted to perfection. Unlike the

50. Sea oats hold sand in place. They were once cut for their graceful beauty but are now protected. Photo by Nicholas Bouler.

51. A natural statue of wind-twisted pine at Grayton Beach State Park, where a nature trail offers a tour of undisturbed shore. Photo by Jean Lufkin Bouler.

California coast, where the Pacific gouges boulders out of the shore, or the Caribbean, where island mountains plunge into the sea, the land here ends in a terrace of sand slipping gently into the water, like a graceful swimmer's shallow dive.

A series of unique twists of nature produce this stunning shore of snow white sand and emerald green water. While other sand beaches generally are composed of various minerals in shades of grays and tans, the white sand at the Emerald Coast is clear quartz. It came from quartz boulders that chipped off the Appalachian Mountains at the end of the last ice age. Huge chunks of rock were gradually ground into smaller pieces as mighty rivers carried them south. The bits of quartz flowed into the Gulf when the sea level was much lower, placing the beach thirty to thirty-five miles south of the current shore.

As temperatures warmed, ice melted and the runoff raised the sea level of the Gulf. Over thousands of years, waves nudged the quartz sand toward shore, while mincing it into smaller and smaller pieces. By the time it was deposited on the coast, forming the beach, it had been ground as fine as sugar.[7]

Unusual sand configurations were constructed. A string of barrier islands and sand spits paralleling the Emerald Coast were probably formed about four thousand to six thousand years ago. These sand formations along the Emerald Coast are part of two thousand miles of barrier islands along coastlines of the United States. Such islands, however, are rare worldwide, with less than 3 percent of coasts around the globe sheltered by them.[8]

The water here appears green because of another series of forces. More than 150 rivers flow into the Gulf. But none empty their murky silt directly into this section. An uneven terrain of sinks and rises—created ages earlier, when the sea level was higher—diverts rivers from flowing into the Gulf at the Emerald Coast. Because the water is unclouded by river sediment, it gains a green color when sunlight reflects off the white sandy bottom.[9]

The setting of this stunning shore seems tranquil. A few plump white clouds drift in a Monet-blue sky. Leaves faintly rustle in a soft breeze, while a dragonfly hovers over a thick-leafed scrub oak.

52. The rhizomes of sea oats dig down three feet and thus anchor dunes. Photo by Jean Lufkin Bouler.

53. At Lake Stalworth, stabilized dunes allow for more complex vegetation, which in turn provides protection for the dunes. Photo by Jean Lufkin Bouler.

As one walks down to the beach for a closer look, the sand crunches and squeaks underfoot. A jogger running at the edge of the surf barely leaves footprints because the fine-textured sand packs into a dense, hard surface. At other beaches, where sand is coarser, the runner would leave more pronounced prints because the larger grains would be more loosely bound and more porous.

A three-foot track, rippled like the print of a tractor tire tread, looks like the mark of a beach-sweeping bulldozer. But instead of running parallel to the sea, this path emerges from the Gulf and returns to the waves—evidence that a three-hundred-pound loggerhead turtle crawled ashore in the cover and coolness of night to lay her eggs in the sand.

Swimming hundreds of miles, this female turtle returned to the beach where she was born. Just how she found her way "home" is unclear. Researchers suspect she was guided by an internal compass that senses the earth's tilt, or perhaps by biological sensors that pick up smells and sounds, the unique feel of certain water currents, or even the earth's magnetic fields.

Sea turtles have inhabited Earth for two hundred million years but are now in danger of disappearing. Over the last two centuries, they have been nearly wiped out—hunted for their eggs or snagged by shrimp nets before protective laws were enacted.[10]

54. Channels from the Gulf cut through sand to create seventeen rare coastal lakes along the Emerald Coast. Photo by Jean Lufkin Bouler.

They have endured cruelty through the ages. In 1876, the poet Sidney Lanier described the sport of turning turtles on their backs when they came out of the water to lay their eggs, one turtle after another all along the beach. Lanier poked fun at another writer, believed to be Thomas Ashe, who a hundred years earlier had sorrowfully recounted a similar sight of overturned turtles about to be butchered "crying" at their funerals. Glands near their eyes that were secreting salt produced the "tears."[11]

Now, with pressure mounting to save the turtles, those that come ashore could very well be met by Eglin researchers, Boy Scouts, and other volunteers who try to protect the nests and help hatchlings safely reach the sea.

Only the female comes ashore, in summer, after reaching maturity—which she gains when she is twelve to thirty years old. She rides in on waves, then pushes through the sand with flippers, sniffing the shore along the way. Her ten-inch head—large for her body, too big to retract into her shell—lifts as she looks around with nearsighted eyes. Once she decides on a spot, she wiggles her reddish-brown shell into the beach as her flippers furiously sweep at the sand, digging a shallow crater to settle into. Her rear flippers dig a deeper pit for the hundred or more eggs she lays over the next hour or so. All done, she pulls the sand back over the nest and crawls through the dark of night into the safety of the sea.[12]

About two months later, bacteria has destroyed some of the eggs. Yet those that survive scratch through their eggshells. When the time comes for these two-inch hatchlings to make their way down the beach to the water, they still face low odds of surviving. Fewer than one in a hundred will live long enough to lay their own eggs. Raccoons, pelicans, and seagulls grab some. Waiting until night, the hatchlings climb out of their sand nest and scramble toward the brightest part of the sky. It is certain death if they mistake houselights for moonlight.

Shaped like tiny birds splayed on the sand, dozens scurry for the Gulf, crawling into the water, flapping flippers, diving to flow with the undertow out beyond the breakers. They swim for up to two days, latch onto a clump of sea grass for a meal of plankton and snails, and begin a cycle that a quarter of a century later carries them back to the same beach.[13]

Another environment exists where green waves slosh onto white sand and fizzle into spent foam. Plants and animals that live here cope with a dramatic world that changes every few seconds, swinging from scorching sun one minute to a flood of salty water the next. When each wave recedes, the cycle starts all over again.[14]

These animals survive by using a variety of tricks to adjust. Some dig tunnels to get to water when the sand is dry. The tiny wedge-shaped mollusk called coquina digs into the soaked sand between each wave. A long-legged, long-billed sanderling tries to pluck the coquina when a spent wave leaves the mollusk exposed. But a lifesaving feature of the coquina thwarts the bird. Each coquina has a slightly different colored shell. When the sanderling pauses for a second, confused by the variety, the coquina dips down and disappears into the sand to safety.

Overhead, beautiful birds add interest to the sky. A pelican the color of nutmeg soars silently on wings that can spread up to seven feet, then folds them halfway and dive bombs to sea. His breast hits the surface so hard it stuns a fish that he scoops up with a beak nearly as long as his body and puts into a throat pouch that strains water from the catch.[15] Another pelican floats on the water, its breast full of air. Schools of mullet shadow the waves, while blue crabs patrol the shallow bottom.

On the inland side of the Grayton Beach dunes, a nature trail winds through still another shore environment. Some 123 plants are listed as native to Grayton Beach. Many of them were eaten or used in various ways by Native

55. A channel from Lake Stalworth at Dune Allen Beach attracts a reddish egret. The Emerald Coast is popular among bird-watchers because the area attracts many migrating species. Photo by Jean Lufkin Bouler.

Americans. Yucca roots, for example, were eaten, and the stalks were woven into baskets. Other Grayton Beach plants include rosemary, deer's tongue, lamb's quarter, rabbit bells, star rush, poor Joe, diamond flower, rock rose, seaside evening primrose, sand squares, and shoe buttons.[16]

Lizards, snakes, skunks, and ghost crabs leave their trails across a mound of bare sand that is moving too fast for plants to grow on. Compact myrtle oaks, dwarfed by salt and wind, grow leathery leaves that are tough and thick to retain water. Their branches, mottled with gray lichen, drop acorns that litter the sandy ground.

The Grayton Beach trail winds beneath a tangled canopy of short live oaks, magnolias, and hickories that look like shrubs with only their tops protruding from the sand. Beyond the trail, oaks grow in a thicket too dense to penetrate, branches scraping against each other in a breeze, creaking like a porch swing. Live oaks grow in abundance here, their limbs stretching up to forty feet from their trunks. The extremely dense wood was prized for shipbuilding in the 1800s and was critical to the new country's national defense, providing timbers for navy ships.[17]

Forests of live oaks used to shade the Emerald Coast, their trunks as rough and rutted as a gator's hide. Even though the live oaks were plentiful on this southernmost border, federal officials feared a nationwide shortage. Building just one ship took more than six hundred trees.[18] In one of the first national steps to conserve a natural resource, the government in 1829 bought a large tract of live oaks on Santa Rosa Sound east of Pensacola, where Gulf Breeze is today.[19] Another forest, near East Pass at Destin, was set aside in 1842 as Moreno Point Military Reservation.

The curved live oak branches that grow almost parallel to the ground, and even the roots spreading under the tree, gave shipwrights shapely lines to cut and plane into bowed hulls. The dark-brown branches weighed a hefty seventy-five pounds per cubic foot. The strength of that wood was made legendary in "Old Ironsides," the battleship USS *Constitution* in the War of 1812, which got its nickname because enemy cannonballs bounced off its sides.[20]

Rot resistant, as well as strong, live oak ships could be counted on to last for years, and timber cut from these trees could be stockpiled for decades underwater. When Old Ironsides was being restored in the 1920s, some of the wood came from live oak logs that had been stored for almost seventy years at the Pensacola Naval Air Station.[21]

56. The spreading limbs of live oaks add beauty to the landscape. They were prized and protected for shipbuilding in the 1800s. Enemy cannonballs bounced off "Old Ironsides." Photo by
Jean Lufkin Bouler.

57. Boaters explore Western Lake at Grayton Beach. The lake is a nursery for insects, fish, birds, and other creatures. Photo by Jean Lufkin Bouler.

During the Civil War, supply lines were broken, and boatbuilders were unable to get wood. They retooled shipbuilding and, instead of using wood, began making ships of iron, ending the era of live oak vessels.[22]

Across Western Lake, on the north side of Grayton Beach, an entirely different tree, the red cedar, gives off a refreshing scent that mixes with sea air near campgrounds where visitors from Europe are among those who visit in the fall and winter. Drawn to the lovely setting, a retired German dentist has been coming here for years. Another man, a young Swede traveling with his girlfriend and visiting the region for the first time, said he just might stay.

The path of the nature trail curves by the banks of Western Lake, made brackish by saltwater carried in by the channel that opens to the Gulf, bringing flounder, mullet, redfish, and drum to the lake. It is one of seventeen rare coastal dune lakes in Walton County separated from the Gulf by beaches and dunes.[23] A saltwater marsh of tall black needle rush nurtures hermit, fiddler, and blue crabs, which along with other marine life feed otters, herons, and raccoons.

A level forest of slash pines, called a flatwood, dwarfs the rest of the landscape. The land in the forest is so flat that rainfall stands, soaking slowly into the sand because a layer of hard-packed subsoil limits the amount of water that can be absorbed.[24]

Bright green fans and thick gray stalks of saw palmetto cover the forest floor. Small-leafed yaupon hollies give more texture to the landscape and are reminders of Sam Story and other Native Americans who used the plant to make "black drink"—similar to tea or coffee.

Grayton Beach State Park—a precious land showcasing the Emerald Coast's magnificent natural heritage—provides a view of how this coast looked hundreds of years ago, a living picture of a natural world undisturbed by humans.

Places to Visit

Gulf Island National Seashore, between Navarre Beach and Pensacola on Santa Rosa Island.

Naval Live Oaks Area, exhibits and trails, Gulf Islands National Seashore Visitor Center, U.S. Highway 98 near Gulf Breeze.

Grayton Beach State Park, 2,228 acres including lake and Gulf-front natural area, County Road 30-A.

Topsail Hill Preserve State Park, County Road 30-A, Santa Rosa Beach.

Deer Lake State Park, County Road 30-A, Santa Rosa Beach.

Henderson Beach State Park, U.S. Highway 98.

Perdido Key State Park, fifteen miles southwest of Pensacola off Highway 292.

St. Andrews State Park, Panama City, from U.S. Highway 98, turn south on Thomas Drive to State Park Lane.

Books to Read

Atlantic and Gulf Coasts (Audubon Society Nature Guide), by William H. Amos and Stephen H. Amos (New York: Knopf, 1985).

Florida Wildflowers and Roadside Plants, by C. Ritchie Bell and Bryan J. Taylor (Chapel Hill, N.C.: Laurel Hill Press, 1982).

Beachcomber's Guide to Gulf Coast Marine Life: Florida, Alabama, Mississippi, Louisiana, and Texas, by Nick Fotheringham and Susan Brunenmeister (Houston: Gulf Publishing Company, 1989).

Live Oaking: Southern Timbers for Tall Ships, by Virginia Steele Wood (Boston: Northeastern University Press, 1981).

11. Backwater Country

On a sunny Saturday morning in the middle of May, Donald Ware cruised the tidal marsh of Hogtown Bayou on the Choctawhatchee Bay eagerly searching for birds. This bayou is especially exciting for birding because the habitat is nearly inaccessible. Ware's boat passed marsh-grass meadows that attract thousands of migrating birds.

This backwater country, the part of the Emerald Coast inland from the beach, is marked by complex ecosystems of wetlands and uplands. Hogtown Bayou and other wetlands are a sprawling maze of waterways that saturate the soil where this coastal land slopes down to meet and merge with the sea. In contrast, uplands offer arid scrub and longleaf pine forests. Exotic plants and rare animals thrive in both of these important environments. Although it is often upstaged by the dazzling beach, this backwater country provides essential habitat for wildlife as well as spectacular scenery.

On his outing at Hogtown Bayou, Ware gazed through his new Zeiss binoculars and to his delight spotted nine seaside sparrows and five least bitterns. The bayou is one of the few places left on the Emerald Coast where these birds can be found. Ware described the scene, making it clear why this area is so attractive to bird-watchers: "Rails were calling from the grass and osprey were soaring overhead looking for fish."[1]

This habitat is so significant to birds that the Audubon Society conducts counts twice a year. By foot, bike, and boat, volunteers cover more than five hundred miles to count birds in Walton and Okaloosa counties. From five-thirty in the morning until six o'clock in the afternoon, members of the Choctawhatchee Audubon Society peer through binoculars in the bright sun or in a light drizzle, looking for the yellow bill of a cuckoo, the red eyes of a vireo, or the brown feathers of a thrasher.

Each sighting is logged and entries are totaled. One outing by the Choctawhatchee Audubon Society found 493 mockingbirds, 4 loons, 491 laughing gulls, 3 purple finches, a purple gallinule, and 475 purple martins. In all, they counted 3,077 birds representing 99 species. Three bald eagles were sighted; one had built a nest at Rocky Bayou, and eggs have hatched there each spring for more than five years.

Volunteers like Ware count again every year in September to record migratory patterns. One fall, a short-tailed hawk and a rare Canada warbler were spotted.[2] Christmas wraps up the yearly Audubon census. The holiday bird count was started in 1900 by ornithologist Frank Chapman to protest a common traditional "Christmas hunt" in which teams competed to shoot the most birds. Chapman organized twenty-seven friends in twenty-five areas, from Canada to California, to count the winged animals instead of shooting them. Now each Christmas more than forty-five thousand enthusiasts take part in 1,650 counts around the globe, from Canada to the Pacific Islands, where North American birds fly for winter.[3]

Compiling data from the spring, fall, and Christmas counts gives information not only about the population of the various bird species, some of which are now endangered, but also about the health of the environment in general.[4]

58. This pond with water lilies is one of the wetlands throughout the Emerald Coast that filters pollution and provides breeding grounds and migratory stopovers for many species. Photo by Jean Lufkin Bouler.

59. A water lily opens at dawn on a pond near Grayton Beach. The fragrant flowers close at night and on cloudy days. By permission of the Williams Gallery, DeFuniak Springs, Fla.

The condition of Emerald Coast wetlands is vital because they provide a host of habitats for other wildlife in addition to birds. Most shellfish and fish caught commercially rely on marshes at one time or another to breed, to escape from predators, or to migrate.

The wetlands provide a critical link in the food chain. Flowering underwater sea grasses attract algae and small animals that are eaten by other animals. The water-loving grasses catch more sediment as the plants grow. Bacteria and tiny organisms break down plant foliage and stems into rich decay, which is eaten by insects. Dragonflies, for example, feed here and lay their eggs on underwater stems. The food chain lengthens as the dragonflies and other insects attract birds and small fish that in turn are food for larger animals.

Alligators, the kings of the wetlands, reign at the top of this food chain. Dating back to the age of the dinosaur, gators up to nine feet long live in Emerald Coast marshes and on creek banks, mostly in freshwater habitats. They emerge in March after six months of hibernating in deep holes.

Alligators come alive at night. Slipping through water, able to stay submerged because they can close a valve in their throat, they cruise for prey to snatch from the bank. Their steel-strength jaws and sharp teeth can grip a deer or cow and pull it underwater in seconds. New teeth, as many as three thousand over a lifetime, grow to replace those lost when attacking prey.

Wetlands such as these on the Emerald Coast once were viewed as almost worthless. By the mid-1800s, the federal government was giving wetlands away—sixty-five million acres to states to fill for crops or to drain and cut timber. Millions of acres have been destroyed nationally, making those that remain along the Emerald Coast all the more precious. Wetlands in the United States today amount to less than half of what Europeans encountered in the 1500s.[5]

Now though, in addition to their value as habitats, the wetlands are recognized as important filters of polluted waters. They trap sediments and provide nurseries and feeding grounds. Some of the wetlands along the Emerald Coast have been designated as official wildlife areas in an increasing nationwide trend to protect wetlands. They are now considered so valuable that experiments are underway to create man-made restorations.[6]

60. W. A. White's shrimp boat, the *Valerie Amanda,* docked at Point Washington on Choctawhatchee Bay. He built the boat in thirteen months, the last of many that he constructed over his lifetime after watching boatbuilders in Destin as a young man. Photo by Jean Lufkin Bouler.

W. A. White's shrimp boat, the *Valerie Amanda,* long docked at Point Washington on Choctawhatchee Bay, was evidence of the value of wetlands to individual families. Born in 1918, White spent a lifetime earning a living off these waterways. The wetlands area was crucial to him: "I was born and raised here," he said in an interview aboard his boat. "I went to school right here [at Point Washington], up to the third grade. I used to have a big seafood market. I imagine I sold ten thousand bags of oysters and no telling how much other seafood."[7]

White, who has since passed away, built his own boats. He named the *Valerie Amanda* for two of his great-grandchildren. "I built the rigging by hand," he said. He boasted that the boat, which he built in thirteen months, could carry sixty blocks of ice that were three hundred pounds each. "She's rated at thirty-five tons," he said. "I built lots of boats. I learned by just standing on the hill watching the Norwegians in Destin until I got it in my mind just how to do it. The Norwegians and Greeks built small seine boats that could get in and out of the Gulf through East Pass."

White outfitted the *Valerie Amanda* with a hundred-year-old ship wheel and an old barber chair for the captain's perch. His fondness for the boat was evident as he pointed to two bunks and to barrels holding water for the kitchen sink and shower, which was a short hose with a showerhead: "I can stay eighteen days without coming in." He was also proud of a fifteen-hundred-dollar EPIRN satellite system to show the location of the boat in an emergency.

Life on the water was good: "I sold shrimp as low as eight cents a pound. I raised my younguns, four boys and a girl." He was a success as a fisherman and a father, even though his shrimp "never got over thirty-five cents a pound." He preferred to see the bright side of things: "We thought we were set."

He shrimped from Apalachicola to Pensacola, but Point Washington was the home he loved. In 1950, White bought two and a half acres at Point Washington for eighteen hundred dollars. The bay was bountiful. Pulling two nets, he caught eight hundred to a thousand pounds a day. He and two other fishermen once caught seventy-five speckled trout: "It took the three of us to hold them up on a string," he recalled.

"This used to be a plumb town. Houses, store," he said pointing to the surrounding landscape at Point Washington, which is mostly marsh now. "This looked like a city." Boats delivered food to the community. Big schooners,

61. W. A. White, born and raised at Point Washington, spent a lifetime earning a living on these waterways. He owned a seafood market where he sold thousands of pounds of oysters, shrimp, and fish. Photo by Jean Lufkin Bouler.

their decks loaded with lumber, sailed from Point Washington to Pensacola, where the wood was then shipped overseas. Dock pilings still stand where a ferry ran from Point Washington across the bay until 1940.

White recalled a torrential storm in the 1920s that drastically changed Choctawhatchee Bay, which had been freshwater. Relentless rains caused the bay to rise eight to ten feet. Cows drowned and houses flooded. "We had a four-foot high picket fence back then," recalled White in an oral history. "It was nothing to row a boat right over the fence and right on into the house."[8] The water came up almost to the top of the front door.[9] Boats motored over submerged highways. Fish were carried by the currents into flooded fields.[10]

Several fishermen in Destin dug a trench to the Gulf to ease the overflow, according to local folklore. High waters from the swollen bay rushed through the channel into the Gulf, tearing a wider gap through the sand and creating a new and bigger East Pass. Sand filled the old pass nearby, where the Green Knight liquor store and bar was built. "They said that water went out of there with a terrible roar," said Harvey Casey in an oral history. "It took that sand in that pass and carried it out into the gulf."[11]

When the waters receded, the Gulf tides surged into the bay, making it salty. As a result, ancient live oaks even today are struggling to survive, unable to root in brackish water. Some tap into fresh springwater underground, but others will die, never to be replaced.[12]

The saltwater killed tall grasses that included reef grass, flag grass, and green needle grass. Ducks and some water birds vanished, as did freshwater fish, which were replaced by saltwater species.[13]

Wetlands score the Emerald Coast like capillaries through the human body. In these transition zones, where water meets land, the mix takes many forms—in swamps, marshes, floodplains, and estuaries. Wetlands may be freshwater, saltwater, or brackish. They may be small or large, permanent or seasonal.

Various forces create these wetlands. Storms or tides bring Gulf water over lowlands, leaving salt marshes in their wake. Sinks dip down to the water table and fill to form ponds and lakes. Spillover from streams and rivers or leaks from beaver dams spread over the ground.

Among the most prominent wetlands of the Emerald Coast are swamps, such as those that soak the land along the Choctawhatchee River. Cypresses more than a hundred feet tall stand in the floodplains. These towering trees

62. Marsh grasses that fringe wetlands nourish a host of marine life. Photo by Jean Lufkin Bouler.

have a long history as the oldest tree species on earth, dating back more than a million years. A single tree can live to be six thousand years old. They grow at a snail's pace, barely six inches in diameter in thirty years. Called "the wood eternal," cypress trees resist decay. Wood from Italian cypress was used to build Rome's St. Peter's gates, which lasted for eleven hundred years.[14]

The Emerald Coast backcountry is also dotted with springs that bubble to the surface from an underground limestone grid that looks like Swiss cheese. At thirteen-foot-deep Ponce de Leon Spring in east Walton County, the limestone forms two caves and an underwater bridge. Some springs even have underwater cliffs for scuba divers to explore.

Other interesting formations common in Walton and Okaloosa counties are steepheads, which are steep-sided ravines where sandy soils have collapsed into springs. They contain various ecosystems, ranging from arid uplands to seeping wetlands. Because these ravines remain largely undisturbed, they provide refuge for unusual animals, like some salamander species and plants such as the Florida yew and Panhandle lily. The sides of the ravines are filled with magnolias, oaks, hickories, and sweet bay. At the bottom, where a clear brook flows, are hollies, dogwoods, and beeches with an understory of dense evergreen shrubs, fetterbrush, and swamp azaleas.[15]

Canoeists love the many freshwater streams of the Emerald Coast wetlands. Northwest Florida streams are known for hosting the largest number of freshwater fish species in the state. The Blackwater River remains preserved in its natural state as the river flows through the largest state forest in Florida. The state forest covers 189,848 acres and bears the river's name. The Blackwater has a sand bottom and white sandbars that contrast sharply with the dark, tannin-stained water.

The uplands ecosystem of wiregrass and longleaf pines protected at the Blackwater River State Forest is very different from wetlands. Strangely, fire is important to the longleaf pine and wiregrass ecosystem. Without an occasional blaze, hardwoods such as laurel oaks become dominant by shading pine seeds, which must have sun to germinate. Fire also creates good soil conditions for seeds to sprout. An understory of wiregrass and palmetto are ready-made sources of fuel that burn easily and help spread the fire. Moderate flames do not harm longleaf pines.

Longleaf pines in forests that have frequent fires are more widely spaced, with fewer shrubs and more diverse vegetation in the understory. Lightning

63. Pitcher plants at the Blackwater River State Forest trap insects in their tubes; the insects drown in water at the bottom and are digested by the plant. Photo by Mary Lou Norwood. Courtesy of State Archives of Florida.

strikes usually cause natural fires every three to five years. More thunderstorm days occur in Florida than anywhere else in the country, and the state has more lightning strikes as well.[16] When natural fires do not occur often enough, prescribed burning helps keep the longleaf pine forest alive. Controlled burning maintains the Blackwater River State Forest, the largest remaining longleaf pine and wiregrass ecosystem in the world.

A rare flower found in the forest, the pitcher plant, also requires fire to survive. Burning maintains an environment of abundant sunlight by thinning vegetation that would otherwise shade the flower. After a fire, underground rhizomes of the plant sprout new leaves.

The plant gets its name from the hollow tube formed by its leaves, which resembles a pitcher. The plant "eats" insects by trapping them in water at the bottom of the tube. Pitcher plants grow in bogs and pine flatwoods among sundews, butterworts, and bladderworts, all of which are also carnivorous.

Another type of uplands ecosystem is scrub, which is perhaps the state's most unusual environment. An example of Florida scrub can be seen at Fred Gannon Rocky Bayou State Recreation Area. Frequently found in backwater country, scrub is the opposite of wetlands.

At Rocky Bayou, the contrast between wetlands and the desertlike scrub is dramatic. Instead of soggy soil, the land of scrub is dry and sandy. The ground is unable to retain moisture, so plants are very different from those in swamps and marshes. In scrub, skinny sand pines grow with a sparse understory. The sand pines share with longleaf pines the remarkable characteristic of requiring fire to reproduce. The two-inch cones of sand pines stay closed, keeping seeds inside until the heat from fire pops them open.[17]

Only a few varieties of plants can adapt to the scrub ecosystem. Those that do survive slurp water quickly when it rains and store the moisture for dry days ahead. Among them is the gopher apple, a low-growing shrub of the rose family that produces a fruit eaten by the gopher tortoise. The tortoise has been on earth more than sixty million years but is now threatened with extinction. Gopher tortoises are often called "wildlife landlords" because they share their burrows with frogs, snakes, small mammals, and birds. Some of these cohabiters are themselves rare species, and the burrow is an important protector.

American hollies also can be found in scrub areas, including Rocky Bayou. A plant with wood as white as ivory, holly was once used for piano keys and false teeth. The ground around the plants in scrub areas is marked by S-shaped trails left by skinks and several other kinds of lizards that are said to "swim" through the sand looking for ants and termites.

The milkweed plant that grows at Rocky Bayou might go unnoticed by a visitor, but it is responsible for a colorful spectacle. Milkweeds attract millions of butterflies that swoop to the Emerald Coast every year. At Halloween, the appropriately colored orange and black monarch butterflies flit to the milkweed stalks on a two-thousand-mile migration to flee North American winters. Miraculously, the monarchs show up again in North America every summer. But until the mid-1970s, no one knew where they went for winter.[18]

If not for the passionate pursuit by scientists, notably a zoologist in Canada,

64. Some 120 native plants, ranging from saw palmetto to yuccas with varied shapes and textures, thrive inland at Grayton Beach. Photo by Jean Lufkin Bouler.

the route and mechanics of the unusual butterfly migration might still be unknown. For forty years, Dr. Fred A. Urquhart, a zoologist at the University of Toronto, tried to track the monarch route and find their winter hideaway.

He designed a tiny sticker to tag the butterflies without weighing down their feather-light wings, and he developed a network of volunteers to notify him if they found a marked monarch. Some of the butterflies covered eighty miles in a day, flying ten to thirty miles per hour.

In 1975, a volunteer in Mexico discovered their winter home. He found millions of the orange and black butterflies covering the limbs of evergreens, some breaking from the weight, on the slopes of mountains nine thousand feet high in the Sierra Madre.[19]

Scientists have learned that the monarchs migrate in stages. At points along the way, such as Rocky Bayou, the butterflies lay eggs, depositing them specifically on milkweed leaves. Milkweeds contain toxic chemicals that are transferred to the caterpillars when they hatch and start eating their food plant. Eating this toxic food makes the caterpillars and the butterflies they become bitter pills for predatory birds to swallow. Each generation somehow picks up the flight pattern, taking several generations to go the whole distance.[20] In this process, their body clocks are tuned to the sun so that they save energy in cold months, reproduce in warm ones, and limit migration to sunlight hours.[21]

The Aztecs of ancient Mexico noted the seasonal appearance of these winged creatures by celebrating the God of Spring, Xipe Totec, who according to legend, was said to kiss a butterfly to wake the world from winter.[22] On the Emerald Coast centuries later, the airborne march of the monarchs continues each fall.

While this backwater country of marshes, longleaf pine forests, springs, and scrub might attract fewer tourists than the white beaches and emerald waters of the Gulf, it is every bit as captivating to wildlife and is just as grand in its own right.

This inland landscape joins the wonders of the Gulf and sandy shore in creating a majestic backdrop for a history rich in characters, from ancient tribes to modern celebrities. The land has served each era well, providing seafood, nuts, and berries for prehistoric tribes, fish for anglers, trees for lumbermen, and scenic beauty for tourists.

Humans have left their mark on the coast, from ancient mounds that stood along waterways to the coastal condos of today. Balancing the needs of people with preservation of the environment has been an issue since Native Americans settled the area, and it has only become more important with time. Early tribes cluttered the coastline with piles of oyster shells. Sam Story left because many pioneers failed to understand the importance of conservation. The lumber and turpentine industries ravaged forests to the extent that developers turned their backs on the Panhandle because the landscape was so ugly. Black smoke from train engines destroyed vegetation.

Development drawn by the natural beauty of this coast continues to encroach on the environment. When cruising down Santa Rosa Sound around the turn of the twentieth century, Senator C. W. Jones had predicted, "I prophesy a day when these shores will be teeming with wealthy beauty lovers."[23] Senator Jones's prediction has come true. Development has drastically changed much of the landscape from long stretches of pristine beach to towering high-rises and shopping strips. Animals such as the Choctawhatchee beach mouse and gopher tortoise are in danger of disappearing.

However, preservation efforts have resulted in large tracts of protected land that showcase this spectacular shore. The challenge in the future will be, as it has been for centuries, to use the land wisely and protect the dunes, coastal lakes, marshes, scrub, and forests that make the Emerald Coast special.

Places to Visit

Fred Gannon Rocky Bayou State Recreation Area, Florida Highway 20, Niceville.

Cessna Park, on Hogtown Bayou, County Road 393 north.

Yellow River, bird watching, Eglin Air Force Base.

Blackwater River State Forest and Park, a river noted for canoeing; trails include Jackson Trail; the headquarters is fifteen miles northeast of Milton, off U.S. Highway 90.

Point Washington State Forest, U.S. Highway 98, Santa Rosa Beach, nine miles south of Freeport.

Ponce de Leon Springs State Recreation Area, one-half mile south of U.S. Highway 90 on County Road 181-A.

Naval live oaks preserve, U.S. Highway 98 near Gulf Breeze.

Big Lagoon State Park, ten miles southwest of Pensacola on Gulf Beach Highway, County Road 292-A.

Camp Helen State Park, Panama City Beach Parkway just west of the Phillips Inlet bridge on the Bay County and Walton County line.

Books to Read

Wetlands (Audubon Society Nature Guides), by William A. Niering (New York: Knopf, 1985).

Adventuring in Florida: The Sierra Club Travel Guide to the Sunshine State and the Sea Islands and Okefenoke Swamp of Georgia, by Allen de Hart (San Francisco: Sierra Club Books, 1991).

Ecosystems of Florida, edited by Ronald L. Myers and John J. Ewel (Orlando: University of Central Florida Press, 1990).

Exploring Wild Northwest Florida, by Gil Nelson (Sarasota, Fla.: Pineapple Press, 1995).

Notes

Chapter 1. Pieces of the Past

1. Yulee W. Lazarus, *The Buck Burial Mound,* 4.
2. Ibid., 17.
3. Jeffery M. Mitchem, "Sylvanus T. Walker's Adventures in Florida."
4. Gordon R. Willey, *Archeology of the Florida Gulf Coast,* 198.
5. Vernon James Knight Jr., *The Moundville Expeditions of Clarence Bloomfield Moore,* 1–3, 15.
6. *Harvard Gazette,* May 2, 2003, "Renowned archaeologist Willey dies at 89," www.hno.harvard.edu (accessed March 23, 2004).
7. Peabody Museum, Harvard University, "Pioneers of Southeastern Archaeology: Gordon R. Willey," www.peabodyharvard.edu (accessed March 23, 2004).
8. Lazarus, *Buck Burial,* 3.
9. Ibid., 14.
10. Ibid.
11. Ibid., 17.
12. Ibid.
13. Ibid.
14. Thomas Creek Archaeological District, National Register of Historic Places Nomination Form, 1983, U.S. Department of the Interior, 2–6.
15. Yulee W. Lazarus, *Indians of the Florida Panhandle,* 4.
16. National Geographic Society, *Wonders of the Ancient World,* 242.
17. Jerald T. Milanich, *Archaeology of Precolumbian Florida,* 63.
18. Robin C. Brown, *Florida's First People: 12,000 Years of Human History,* 70.
19. Milanich, *Archaeology,* 98.
20. Brown, *Florida's First People,* 112, 113.
21. National Geographic Society, *Wonders,* 241.
22. Ibid., 250.
23. Willey, *Archeology,* 213.

Chapter 2. European Explorers

1. Cleve Hallenbeck, trans., *Álvar Núñez Cabeza de Vaca: The Journey and Route of the First European to Cross the Continent of North America, 1534–1536,* 4.
2. T. Buckingham Smith, trans., foreword to *Relation of Nuñez Cabeza de Vaca.*
3. Núñez Cabeza de Vaca, Álvar. *Cabeza de Vaca's Adventures in the Unknown Interior of America,* trans. Cyclone Covey, 9.

4. Hallenbeck, *Álvar Núñez*, 17.

5. Covey, *Adventures*, 28, 29.

6. Ibid., 31.

7. Hallenbeck, *Álvar Núñez*, 4.

8. Covey, *Adventures*, 9.

9. Hallenbeck, *Álvar Núñez*, 44.

10. Ibid.

11. Ibid., 45.

12. Ibid., 46, 47.

13. William T. Pilkington, introduction to Covey, *Adventures*.

14. Thomas Jefferson Foundation, "Books on American Geography in Thomas Jefferson's Library," www.monticello.org/jefferson/lewisandclark/americabooks.html (accessed April 14, 2006).

15. Marvin T. Smith, "Indian Responses to European Contact: The Coosa Example," 141.

16. Tommy Smith, *The History of Bay County: From the Beginning*, 99.

17. Charles Hudson, Chester B. DePratter, and Marvin T. Smith, "Hernando de Soto's Expedition through the Southern United States," 81.

18. Virginia Parks, *Pensacola: Spaniards to Space-Age*, 6.

19. Charlton W. Tebeau, *A History of Florida*, 26.

20. Parks, *Pensacola*, 110.

21. Ibid., 7, 11.

22. Tebeau, *History of Florida*, 26.

23. Parks, *Pensacola*, 14.

24. Ibid., 19–22.

25. Milan Tapia, *Spanish Approach to Pensacola, 1689–1693*, 290–91.

26. Pierre le Moyne d'Iberville, *Iberville's Gulf Journals*, 29, 32.

27. Parks, *Pensacola*, 24.

28. Marjory Stoneman Douglas, *Florida: The Long Frontier*, 101.

29. Parks, *Pensacola*, 30.

30. Ibid., 32.

31. William Bartram, *Travels and Other Writings*, 337.

32. Parks, *Pensacola*, 34, 36.

33. William James Wells, *Pioneering in the Panhandle*, 225.

34. Albert James Pickett, *History of Alabama*, 410.

35. Parks, *Pensacola*, 37.

36. Tebeau, *History of Florida*, 95.

37. Pickett, *History of Alabama*, 422.

38. Douglas, *Florida*, 117.

39. Scottish Studies Foundation, "Scots around the World," www.electricscotland.com/history/world/pantonleslie.htm (accessed April 14, 2006).

40. Tebeau, *History of Florida*, 96.

41. Scottish Studies Foundation, "Scots around the World."

42. Pickett, *History of Alabama*, 470.

Chapter 3. Sam Story and the Scots

1. John L. McKinnon, *History of Walton County,* 13.
2. Ibid., 16, 62.
3. Charles Hudson, *The Southeastern Indians,* 378.
4. McKinnon, *History of Walton County,* 14, 26.
5. Bernard Romans, *A Concise Natural History of East and West Florida,* 275.
6. Ibid., 82.
7. Ibid., 79.
8. Tebeau, *History of Florida,* 134.
9. Virginia Parks, *Christmas in Old Pensacola,* 3.
10. Catharine L. Stewart and Maude Hollowell, *Old Customs of Pensacola and Favorite Recipes of the Times,* 4.
11. Parks, *Pensacola,* 61.
12. Stewart and Hollowell, *Old Customs,* 4.
13. McKinnon, *History of Walton County,* 14.
14. Ibid., 11, 13.
15. Parks, *Pensacola,* 45.
16. Ibid., 45, 43.
17. Ibid., 48.
18. Ibid., 49, 51.
19. Julie Massoni, *Camp Pinchot,* 5.
20. McKinnon, *History of Walton County,* 13.
21. Romans, *Concise Natural History,* 128, 129.
22. McKinnon, *History of Walton County,* 15.
23. Ibid., 16.
24. Ibid., 16, 17, 18, 34.
25. Bartram, *Travels,* 316–17.
26. McKinnon, *History of Walton County,* 17.
27. Ibid., 22.
28. Ibid., 33.
29. Ibid., 46, 61.
30. Brad Hartman, "Plants," xxvii.
31. Destin Fishing Museum.
32. McKinnon, *History of Walton County,* 21, 23, 119.
33. University of Florida, Bureau of Economic and Business Research, www.bebr.ufl.edu/Publications/Hist_Census_Counties.pdf (accessed December 13, 2006).
34. McKinnon, *History of Walton County,* 55, 30.
35. Ibid., 150.
36. Ibid., 64.
37. Ibid., 60–62.
38. Ibid., 72–76.
39. Ibid., 75, 82–83.
40. Ibid., 89.
41. Ibid., 95, 98.
42. Ibid., 118.

43. Brian R. Rucker, "West Florida's Creek Indian Crisis of 1837," 317, 319.

44. Marlene Womack, *Along the Bay: A Pictorial History of Bay County,* 31, 19.

45. Rucker, "Creek Crisis," 321.

46. Ibid.

47. McKinnon, *History of Walton County,* 109.

48. Rucker, "Creek Crisis," 326.

49. Ibid., 327.

50. Ibid., 327, 328.

51. Ibid., 330, 331, 334.

52. Parks, *Pensacola,* 52.

53. Michael Gannon, *Florida,* 28.

54. Parks, *Pensacola,* 54.

55. Pickett, *History of Alabama,* 28.

56. Smith, *History of Bay County,* 99.

57. Marlene Womack, *The Bay Country of Northwest Florida,* 1.

58. Smith, *History of Bay County,* 106.

59. Womack, *Along the Bay,* 17.

Chapter 4. Leonard Destin's Fishing Legacy

1. Vivian Foster Mettee, *Destin History: . . . And the Roots Run Deep,* 44a.

2. Leonard Patrick Hutchinson, *History of the Playground Area,* 44.

3. Junior Service League Fort Walton Beach, *Recollections,* 7.

4. Destin Fishing Museum, videotape.

5. Ibid.

6. Mettee, *Destin History,* 29.

7. Ibid.

8. Gene M. Burnett, *Florida's Past: People and Events That Shaped the State,* 179.

9. Parks, *Pensacola,* 60.

10. Ibid., 59.

11. Ibid., 58.

12. Ibid., 62.

13. Albert James Pickett, *Letters from Pensacola, Descriptive and Historical (1858),* 28.

14. Nathaniel H. Bishop, *Four Months in a Sneakbox,* 252.

15. Ibid.

16. Ibid, 253–259.

17. Bruce Rolfsen, "Destin's Heritage Lies in Tradition of the Sea," 22.

18. Muriel Destin, telephone interview with author, August 19, 2004.

19. Ibid.

20. Junior Service League, *Recollections,* 3.

21. Steve Tuthill, former director of the Indian Temple Mound Museum, interview with author, April 16, 1995, Fort Walton Beach, Fla.

22. Bureau of Economic and Business Research, Warrington College of Business, University of Florida, "Historical Census Counts for Florida and Its Counties, 1830 through 2000," www.bebr.ufl.edu/Publications/Hist_Census_Counties.pdf (accessed April 21, 2006).

23. Hutchinson, *History,* 44.

24. Mettee, *Destin History,* 38, 94.

25. Willie Mae Marler Taylor, interview with the author, April 15, 1996, Destin, Fla.

26. William Columbia Pryor, "The Most Unforgettable Character I've Met: Portrait of a Fast-Disappearing Breed," 133.

27. Ibid., 135.

28. Ibid., 132, 134, 136.

29. Ibid., 133, 132, 135.

30. Ibid., 134.

31. Ibid., 136; Mettee, *Destin History,* 37.

32. Mettee, *Destin History,* 23.

33. Destin Fishing Museum, exhibit.

34. Ibid.

35. James H. Cason, Robert A. Mills, and Paula A. Tully, *Historical Remembrances of Choctawhatchee Bay, Northwest Florida,* 42.

36. Mettee, *Destin History,* 29.

37. Cason, Mills, and Tully, *Historical Remembrances of Choctawhatchee Bay,* 3, 6.

38. Ibid., 16.

39. Ibid., 30.

40. Ibid., 42.

Chapter 5. Civil War

1. Hutchinson, *History,* 48, 49.

2. Ibid., 49.

3. McKinnon, *History of Walton County,* 68.

4. J. H. Gilman, "With Slemmer in Pensacola Harbor," 26.

5. Tebeau, *History of Florida,* 187.

6. Hutchinson, *History,* 48.

7. William Watson Davis, *The Civil War and Reconstruction in Florida,* 52.

8. Frank Edward Kittredge, *The Man with the Branded Hand,* 12.

9. Parks, *Pensacola,* 63.

10. Kittredge, *Branded Hand,* 13.

11. Parks, *Pensacola,* 63.

12. Kittredge, *Branded Hand,* 16.

13. Ibid., 16, 17.

14. Ibid., 17, 18.

15. Jonathan Walker, *The Branded Hand: Trial and Imprisonment of Jonathan Walker,* 8–21.

16. McKinnon, *History of Walton County,* 181.

17. Ibid., 181, 184, 191.

18. Ibid., 217, 218.

19. Ibid., 217, 218, 220.

20. Davis, *Civil War,* 53, 55.

21. Ibid., 62–63.

22. Gilman, "With Slemmer," 27.

23. Tebeau, *History of Florida,* 201.

24. Gilman, "With Slemmer," 27.

25. Ibid.

26. Tebeau, *History of Florida,* 178.

27. Davis, *Civil War,* 62, 63.

28. Ibid.

29. Ibid.

30. Gilman, "With Slemmer," 29.

31. Ibid.

32. Ibid.

33. Board of State Institutions, *Soldiers of Florida in the Seminole Indian, Civil, and Spanish-American Wars,* 35–37.

34. Shelby Foote, *The Civil War: A Narrative, Fort Sumpter to Perryville,* 112, 113.

35. Hutchinson, *History,* 51.

36. Gilman, "With Slemmer," 32.

37. Board of State Institutions, *Soldiers of Florida,* 38.

38. Gilman, "With Slemmer," 32.

39. McKinnon, *History of Walton County,* 68.

40. Hutchinson, *History,* 50–51.

41. Alexander McDonald, letter dated December 29, 1861, at Valparaiso Heritage Museum.

42. John L. to John Newton, April 2, 1862, University of West Florida Special Collections Department.

43. Davis, *Civil War,* 257–58.

44. Rolfsen, "Destin's Heritage," 22.

45. Newton letters, dated January 31, 1864, to Sisters and dated September 28, 1868, to Daniel. University of West Florida Special Collections.

46. Parks, *Pensacola,* 71.

47. Board of State Institutions, *Soldiers of Florida,* 63, 75.

48. Tebeau, *History of Florida,* 223.

49. Ibid., 209–211.

50. Foote, *Civil War,* 353.

51. George F. Pearce, *Pensacola during the Civil War: A Thorn in the Side of the Confederacy,* 219; Davis, *Civil War,* 312.

52. Davis, *Civil War,* 311, 312.

53. Mark Derr, *Some Kind of Paradise: A Chronicle of Man and the Land in Florida,* 303; Bruce Rolfsen, "Quiet Walton Hamlet Had Its Roots in Lumber," 100.

54. Harold W. Bell, *Glimpses of the Panhandle,* 39.

55. Womack, *Bay Country,* 16.

56. Smith, *History of Bay County,* 48, 108.

57. Womack, *Bay Country,* 23.

58. Bell, *Glimpses,* 36.

59. Charles Ledyard Norton, *Handbook of Florida,* 365; Womack, *Bay Country,* 21–23.

60. Tebeau, *History of Florida,* 217.

61. Jane R. Griffing, "Letters from Florida," *Boston Republic,* 1883.

62. George M. Barbour, *Florida for Tourists, Invalids, and Settlers,* 72–77. Information in the following paragraphs is from this source.

63. *McGraw Election Railway Manual,* McGraw Publishing Company, 1984.

Chapter 6. Sawmills and Turpentine Stills

1. Rolfsen, "Quiet Walton," *Our Town,* 102.

2. *Eden State Gardens* (pamphlet), 2; *Eden Mansion—Gardens* (pamphlet).

3. Rolfsen, "Quiet Walton," 102.

4. Massoni, *Camp Pinchot,* 9.

5. *Eden State Gardens,* 2.

6. Ibid.

7. Massoni, *Camp Pinchot,* 9.

8. Romans, *Concise Natural History,* 124, 142.

9. Junior Service League, *Recollections,* 8.

10. Douglas, *Florida,* 241.

11. Tebeau, *History of Florida,* 282.

12. Parks, *Pensacola,* 78, 81.

13. Tebeau, *History of Florida,* 282.

14. Pearce, *Pensacola during the Civil War,* epilogue.

15. Burnett, *Florida's Past,* 100.

16. Parks, *Pensacola,* 75.

17. Derr, *Some Kind of Paradise,* 114.

18. Parks, *Pensacola,* 78.

19. Pensacola Historical Society, *The Golden Dream: Life in Pensacola in the 1870s,* 27.

20. Parks, *Pensacola,* 80.

21. Ibid., 79, 82.

22. Smith, *History of Bay County,* 48.

23. Womack, *Bay Country,* 2.

24. Bell, *Glimpses,* 103.

25. Robert S. Blount, *Spirits of Turpentine: A History of Naval Stores, 1528–1950,* 1.

26. Wells, *Pioneering,* 102.

27. Blount, *Spirits,* 17, 25.

28. Wells, *Pioneering,* 95.

29. Blount, *Spirits,* 36.

30. Wells, *Pioneering,* 93, 94.

31. Blount, *Spirits,* 19, 38, 39.

32. Wells, *Pioneering,* 94.

33. Blount, *Spirits,* 39.

34. Wells, *Pioneering,* 95, 96.

35. Blount, *Spirits,* 41.

36. Ibid., 30, 36.

37. Stetson Kennedy, *Palmetto Country,* 262.

38. Womack, *Bay Country,* 175.

39. Blount, *Spirits,* 19, 45.
40. Massoni, *Camp Pinchot,* 15.
41. Ibid., 2, 14.
42. Blount, *Spirits,* 2.
43. Parks, *Pensacola,* 85.
44. Derr, *Some Kind of Paradise,* 114.

Chapter 7. Railroads: Gateway to the Gulf

1. David Woodward, "The L&N and DeFuniak Springs," 5.
2. *Heritage Herald,* 2.
3. Woodward, "L&N," 4, 5.
4. *Heritage Herald,* 1.
5. "How Defuniak Springs Acquired Its Name," 2.
6. Mrs. P. L. Biddle, "Early Days of DeFuniak Springs, Fla."
7. *The Florida Chautauqua,* 1.
8. Woodward, "L&N," 5.
9. Dean DeBolt, "The Florida Chautauqua: An Overview of Its History and Its Cultural Impact on West Florida," 114.
10. Ibid., 115.
11. Woodward, "L&N," 7.
12. Ibid., 6.
13. Ibid., 8.
14. *Heritage Herald,* 2.
15. *Florida Chautauqua,* 1.
16. Photos, L&N.
17. "DeFuniack Springs Back," 18–22.
18. Hotel Chautaugua, "The Adirondacks of Western Florida" (pamphlet), 1.
19. Woodward, "L&N," 7.
20. *Florida Chautauqua,* 1.
21. Woodward, "L&N," 6.
22. Oliver Marvin Crosby, *Florida Facts, Both Bright and Blue: A Guide Book to Intending Settlers, Tourists, and Investors from a Northerner's Standpoint; Plain Unvarnished Truth, without "Taffy," No Advertisements or Puffs,* 51.
23. Woodward, "L&N," 7.
24. *History of Walton County, Florida* (pamphlet).
25. Woodward, "L&N," 7.
26. *Heritage Herald,* 1.
27. Exhibit, Walton-DeFuniak Springs Library.
28. *DeFuniak Springs Daily Local,* "The Chautaugua, And Its Doings," March 6, 1894, 1.
29. DeBolt, "Florida Chautauqua," 118.
30. Woodward, "L&N," 9.
31. South Walton Tourist Development Council, *Beaches of South Walton,* 4.
32. Bruce Rolfsen, "Grayton Beach Stakes Its Claim as One of Area's Oldest Towns," 93.
33. Wilfred "Chick" Huettel, "Early Settlements around Hogtown Bayou," 4.

34. Santa Rosa promotional papers, Bayou Arts and Antiques.
35. Ibid.
36. Huettel, "Early Settlements," 5, 10.
37. Ibid., 11.
38. Florida Bureau of Immigration, Department of Agriculture, *All Florida*, 155.
39. Tom Huyck, "Communities Grew with Blueberry Industry," 4.
40. Florida Bureau of Immigration, *All Florida*, 154.
41. Huyck, "Communities Grew," 4.
42. Womack, *Bay Country*, 2.
43. Ibid., 1.
44. Womack, *Along the Bay*, 49.
45. Bell, *Glimpses*, 41.
46. Ibid.
47. Womack, *Bay Country*, 11.
48. Womack, *Along the Bay*, overleaf.
49. Womack, *Bay Country*, 3, 29.
50. Smith, *History of Bay County*, 116.
51. Bell, *Glimpses*, 76.
52. Smith, *History of Bay County*, 8.
53. Womack, *Along the Bay*, overleaf.
54. Smith, *History of Bay County*, 8.
55. Womack, *Bay Country*, 65.
56. Ibid., 99.
57. Bell, *Glimpses*, 36.

Chapter 8. Characters, Celebrities—and Outlaws

1. Junior Service League, *Recollections*, 10, 11.
2. Womack, *Bay Country*, 124.
3. Junior Service League, *Recollections*, 11.
4. Charles Higham, *The Duchess of Windsor: The Secret Life*, 23.
5. Wallis Windsor, *The Heart Has Its Reasons*, 46.
6. Naval Air Station Pensacola, www.naspensacola.navy.mil (accessed June 5, 2005).
7. Parks, *Pensacola*, 91.
8. Real Estate Center, Texas A&M University, www.recenter.tamu.edu (accessed June 8, 2005).
9. Windsor, *Heart*, 46.
10. Ibid., 49.
11. Ibid., 50, 51.
12. Ibid., 51.
13. F. F. Bingham, *Log of the Peep of the Day: Summer Cruises in West Florida Waters, 1912–1915*, 3.
14. Tracy Wenzel, "Mail Left on Mary Esther," 40.
15. Bingham, *Log of the Peep*, 6, 14.
16. Ibid., 14.

17. Windsor, *Heart,* 52.

18. Ibid., 56.

19. Stephen Birmingham, *Duchess: The Story of Wallis Warfield Windsor,* 18.

20. Windsor, *Heart,* 63, 64.

21. Birmingham, *Duchess,* 19.

22. Ibid., 19–26, 27.

23. Ibid., 36, 49, 50.

24. Ibid., 54, 55, 50.

25. Windsor, *Heart,* 211, 212.

26. Birmingham, *Duchess,* 83, 89, 95, 105, 106.

27. Ibid., 140, 145, 155, 179, 180, 187.

28. Ibid., 199, 201.

29. Parks, *Pensacola,* 85.

30. Destin Fishing Museum, videotape.

31. Mettee, *Destin History,* 32.

32. Ibid., 32, 33.

33. Womack, *Bay Country,* 190.

34. Parks, *Pensacola,* 94.

35. George Fisher, ed., *Historical Remembrances of Choctawhatchee River,* 16, 68.

36. Laurence Bergreen, *Capone: The Man and the Era,* 270, 271.

37. Jeff Newell, "Florosa Gets Name from Inn," 28.

38. Wells, *Pioneering,* 60.

39. Womack, *Bay Country,* 135.

40. Ibid., 130.

41. Pam Golden, "Prosperity, Fame, Disaster Part of Tale of Okaloosa's Hub City," 19.

42. Junior Service League, *Recollections,* 29, 31.

43. Ibid., 31; Don Adams, interview with the author, April 22, 2004, Birmingham, Ala.; Gannon, *Florida,* 107.

44. *Cultural Resources at Eglin AFB* (pamphlet).

45. Junior Service League, *Recollections,* 29, 30.

46. Naval Air Station Pensacola, "History," www.naspensacola.navy.mil/index.cfm/fa/base_info.history (accessed June 5, 2005).

47. Parks, *Pensacola,* 100.

48. Juanealya McCormick Sutton, *The Man behind the Scenes,* 59.

49. Womack, *Along the Bay,* 160.

50. Hank Williams Museum, Georgiana, Ala.

51. Don Adams interview.

52. Chris LaRoche, interview with the author, Valparaiso Heritage Museum, August 12, 1995, Valparaiso, Fla.

53. Tebeau, *History of Florida,* 430.

54. Lee Forst, "FWB Built on Sound Foundation," 32.

55. Air Force Armament Museum, Eglin AFB, exhibit.

56. Naval Air Station Pensacola, "History."

57. Smith, *History of Bay County,* 86.

58. Naval Surface Warfare Center, Panama City, www.ncsc.navy.mil (accessed May 9, 2006).

59. Smith, *History of Bay County,* 58, 67.

60. *Sandestin: The Magazine of the Premier Resort on the Gulf Coast,* 83, 34, 10.

61. Kathryn Ziewitz and June Wiaz, *Green Empire: The St. Joe Company and the Remaking of Florida's Panhandle,* 4.

62. Laszlo Buhasz, "A 'Sea Salt–Glazed Mayberry'" (March 26, 2005), Seaside Office of Marketing and Public Relations, www.seasidefl.com/newsStory.asp?releaseId=1037 (accessed May 12, 2006).

63. Julia Reed, "In Seaside, Fla., Goodbye Stuffed Flounder, Hello Foie Gras" (*New York Times,* October 16, 2005), Seaside Office of Marketing and Public Relations, www.seasidefl.com/newsStory.asp?releaseId=1043 (accessed November 20, 2006).

64. Buhasz, "Sea Salt–Glazed Mayberry."

65. Reed, "In Seaside."

66. Ziewitz and Wiaz, *Green Empire,* 35.

67. Ibid., 5, 3, 45.

68. Ibid., 15.

Chapter 9. World beneath the Waves

1. Quoted in American Association of Petroleum Geologists, *Explorer,* www.aapg.org (accessed July 20, 2005).

2. Emerald Coast Convention and Visitors Bureau, "Northwest Florida's Emerald Coast," www.destin-fwb.com (accessed August 22, 2006).

3. Caleb G. Forshey, *The Physics of the Gulf of Mexico and Its Chief Affluent, The Mississippi River,* 4, 6.

4. Leonard Engel and the Editors of Time-Life Books, *The Sea,* 55.

5. William J. Broad, *The Universe Below: Discovering the Secrets of the Deep Sea,* 59, 60.

6. Bill Kaezor, "New Technology Will Seek Secrets of Gulf," *Birmingham News,* August 9, 2004.

7. Michael Weber, Richard T. Townsend, and Rose Bierce, *Environmental Quality in the Gulf of Mexico: A Citizen's Guide,* 6.

8. Robert H. Gore, *The Gulf of Mexico,* 60.

9. Weber, Townsend, and Bierce, *Environmental Quality,* 7, 9, 10.

10. Gore, *Gulf,* 127; Tracy Louthain, Beaches of South Walton Tourist Development Council, telephone interview with author, December 19, 2006.

11. ScubaTech of Northwest Florida, www.scubatechnwfl.com (accessed May 7, 2006).

12. Gore, *Gulf,* 181–83.

13. Ichthyology at the Florida Museum of Natural History, University of Florida, "Education: Biological Profiles: Tarpon," www.flmnh.ufl.edu/fish/Gallery/Descript/Tarpon/Tarpon.html (accessed May 4, 2006).

14. Weber, Townsend, and Bierce, *Environmental Quality,* 6, 7.

15. Gore, *Gulf,* 164; Broad, *Universe Below,* 18, 24.

16. Gore, *Gulf,* 83, 150, 151, 148, 149.

17. Ibid., 230, 231.

18. Ibid., 143, 154, 84.

19. Laurence G. Barnes, "The Nature of Dolphins," 24–26.

20. Gore, *Gulf*, 217.

21. Ibid., 58–60.

22. Tjeerd H. Van Andel, *Tales of an Old Ocean: Exploring the Deep-Sea World of the Geologist and Oceanographer*, 35, 36.

23. Gore, *Gulf*, 68–73.

24. Ibid., 81.

25. Ibid., 80.

26. Weber, Townsend, and Bierce, *Environmental Quality*, 39.

27. Gore, *Gulf*, 240.

28. Weber, Townsend, and Bierce, *Environmental Quality*, 51.

Chapter 10. Sandy Shore

1. Florida Oceanographic Coastal Center, "Sand Dunes, More Than Piles of Sand," www.floridaoceanographic.org/environ/dunes.html (accessed May 8, 2006).

2. William H. Amos and Stephen H. Amos, *Atlantic and Gulf Coasts*, 67.

3. Amos and Amos, *Atlantic and Gulf Coasts*, 66.

4. Sandra Sneckenberger, U.S. Fish and Wildlife Service, Panama City, e-mail to author, March 22, 2006.

5. Beach to Bay Connection, South Walton Coastal Conservancy, www.beachtobay. org (accessed May 8, 2006).

6. Nigel Nicolson, *Virginia Woolf*, 104.

7. Ruthe Wolverton and Walt Wolverton, *The National Seashores: The Complete Guide to America's Scenic Coastal Parks*, 6–8.

8. Jennifer Ackerman, "Islands at the Edge," 2–31.

9. Brad Pickel, Beaches of South Walton Tourist Development Council, e-mail to author, December 14, 2006.

10. Jeff Ripple, *Sea Turtles*, 20.

11. Sidney Lanier, *Florida: Its Scenery, Climate, and History*, 94–96.

12. Nick Fotheringham and Susan Brunenmeister, *Beachcomber's Guide to Gulf Coast Marine Life: Florida, Alabama, Mississippi, Louisiana, and Texas*, 99–103.

13. Ripple, *Sea Turtles*, 41–44.

14. Amos and Amos, *Atlantic and Gulf Coasts*, 58.

15. Ibid., 576.

16. Grayton Beach State Recreation Area list, "Native Plants."

17. *Naval Live Oaks* (brochure).

18. Virginia Steele Wood, *Live Oaking: Southern Timber for Tall Ships*, 55.

19. *Naval Live Oaks Trail Guide* (brochure).

20. *Naval Live Oaks*.

21. Ibid.

22. *Naval Live Oaks Trail Guide*.

23. Choctawhatchee Basin Alliance, www.basinalliance.org (accessed May 9, 2006).

24. Florida Outdoors, "Upland Habitats: Pine Flatwoods," www.florida-outdoors. com/pine.htm (accessed May 9, 2006).

Chapter 11. Backwater Country

1. Donald Ware, e-mail to author, July 7, 2004.
2. North American Migration Count, Audubon Society, Walton and Okaloosa counties, list of birds sighted May 11, 1996. Compiled by Donald Ware of the Choctawhatchee Audubon Society www.choctawhatcheeaudubon.org.
3. National Audubon Society, "History and Objectives," www.audubon/bird/cbc/history.html (accessed July 7, 2004).
4. Ibid.
5. William A. Niering, *Wetlands,* 18, 19.
6. Ibid., 35.
7. W. A. White, interview with the author, August 8, 1995, Point Washington, Fla. Information in the next several paragraphs is from this interview.
8. Cason, Mills, and Tully, *Historical Rembrances of Choctawhatchee River,* 65, 66.
9. White, interview.
10. Cason, Mills, and Tully, *Historical Remembrances of Choctawhatchee River,* 73.
11. Ibid., 66, 11.
12. Tuthill, interview.
13. Cason, Mills, and Tully, *Historical Remembrances of Choctawhatchee Bay,* 20.
14. Kennedy, *Palmetto Country,* 8.
15. Frank Stephenson, "Panhandle Plainsman" (*Florida State University Research in Review,* fall 2004, 16–33), http://rinr.magnet.fsu.edu/fall2004/documents/fall2004.pdf (accessed November 20, 2006).
16. Ronald L. Myers and John J. Ewel, eds., *Ecosystems of Florida,* 129.
17. Meyers and Ewel, *Ecosystems,* 162.
18. Carl Zimmer, "Monarch Butterflies," 38.
19. Fred A. Urquhart, "Found at Last: The Monarch's Winter Home," 161.
20. Zimmer, "Monarch Butterflies," 38, 39.
21. Urquhart, "Found at Last," 162, 165.
22. Monarch Festival of South Walton, information sheet, Seaside, Fla.
23. McKinnon, *History of Walton County,* 49.

Bibliography

Ackerman, Jennifer. "Islands at the Edge." *National Geographic*. August 1997, 2–31.

Amos, William H., and Stephen H. Amos. *Atlantic and Gulf Coasts*. Audubon Society Nature Guides. New York: Knopf, 1985.

Barbour, George M. *Florida for Tourists, Invalids, and Settlers*. New York: D. Appleton, 1882.

Barnes, Laurence G. "The Nature of Dolphins." In *The Greenpeace Book of Dolphins*, ed. John May. New York: Sterling Publishing, 1990.

Bartram, William. *William Bartram: Travels and Other Writings*. With notes by Thomas P. Slaughter. 1791. Reprint, New York: Library of America, 1996.

Bell, C. Ritchie, and Bryan J. Taylor. *Florida Wildflowers and Roadside Plants*. Chapel Hill, N.C.: Laurel Hill Press, 1982.

Bell, Harold W. *Glimpses of the Panhandle*. Chicago: Adams Press, 1961.

Bergreen, Laurence. *Capone: The Man and the Era*. New York: Simon and Schuster, 1996.

Biddle, Mrs. P. L. "Early Days of DeFuniak Springs, Fla." Paper presented to the Woman's Club, Walton-DeFuniak Springs Library archives.

Bingham, F. F. *Log of the Peep of the Day: Summer Cruises in West Florida Waters, 1912–1915*. Bagdad, Fla.: Patagonia Press, 1991.

Birmingham, Stephen. *Duchess: The Story of Wallis Warfield Windsor*. Boston: Little, Brown, 1981.

Bishop, Nathaniel H. *Four Months in a Sneakbox*. Boston: Lee and Shepard; New York: C. T. Dillingham, 1879.

Blount, Robert S. *Spirits of Turpentine: A History of Naval Stores, 1528–1950*. Tallahassee: Florida Agricultural Museum, 1993.

Board of State Institutions. *Soldiers of Florida in the Seminole Indian, Civil, and Spanish-American Wars*. Macclenny, Fla.: R. J. Ferry, 1983.

Broad, William J. *The Universe Below: Discovering the Secrets of the Deep Sea*. New York: Simon and Schuster, 1997.

Brose, David S., and Nancy Marie White, eds. *Northwest Florida Expeditions of Clarence Bloomfield Moore*. Tuscaloosa: University of Alabama Press, 1999.

Brown, Robin C. *Florida's First People: 12,000 Years of Human History*. Sarasota, Fla.: Pineapple Press, 1994.

Bucker, George E. *Blockaders, Refuges, and Contrabands: Civil War on Florida's Gulf Coast, 1861–1865*. Tuscaloosa: University of Alabama Press, 1993.

Burnett, Gene M. *Florida's Past: People and Events That Shaped the State*. Sarasota, Fla.: Pineapple Press, 1986.

Case, Victoria, and Robert Ormond Case. *We Called It Culture: The Story of Chautauqua.* Garden City, N.Y.: Doubleday, 1948.

Cason, James H., Robert A. Mills, and Paula A. Tully. *Historical Remembrances of Choctawhatchee Bay, Northwest Florida.* Havana, Fla.: Northwest Florida Water Management District, 1985.

Crosby, Oliver Marvin. *Florida Facts, Both Bright and Blue: A Guide Book to Intending Settlers, Tourists, and Investors from a Northerner's Standpoint; Plain Unvarnished Truth, without "Taffy," No Advertisements or Puffs.* New York: n.p., 1887.

Cultural Resources at Eglin AFB. (Pamphlet.)

Davis, William Watson. *The Civil War and Reconstruction in Florida.* New York: Columbia University, 1913.

DeBolt, Dean. "The Florida Chautauqua: An Overview of Its History and Its Cultural Impact on West Florida." In *Threads of Tradition and Culture along the Gulf Coast,* ed. Ronald V. Evans, 110–25. Pensacola: Gulf Coast History and Humanities Conference, 1986.

"DeFuniak Springs Back," *Southern Living,* February 1999, 18–22.

De Hart, Allen. *Adventuring in Florida: The Sierra Club Travel Guide to the Sunshine State and the Sea Islands and Okefenoke Swamp of Georgia.* San Francisco: Sierra Club Books, 1991.

Dennis, John V. *The Great Cypress Swamps.* Baton Rouge: Louisiana State University Press, 1988.

Derr, Mark. *Some Kind of Paradise: A Chronicle of Man and the Land in Florida.* New York: W. Morrow, 1989.

Douglas, Marjory Stoneman. *Florida: The Long Frontier.* New York: Harper and Row, 1967.

Eden Mansion—Gardens. (Pamphlet.) Florida Department of Natural Resources, Division of Recreation and Parks, Tallahassee, Fla.

Eden State Gardens. (Pamphlet.) Florida Department of Natural Resources, Division of Recreation and Parks, Tallahassee, Fla.

Engel, Leonard, and the Editors of Time-Life Books. *The Sea.* New York: Time-Life Books, 1961.

Fisher, George, ed. *Historical Remembrances of Choctawhatchee River.* Havana, Fla.: Northwest Florida Water Management District, 1989.

Florida Bureau of Immigration, Department of Agriculture. *All Florida.* Tallahassee, 1926.

The Florida Chautauqua 1, no. 1 (June 1892).

Florida Game and Freshwater Fish Commission. "Wild Florida." (Pamphlet.) Vol. 1. Florida Game and Freshwater Fish Commission, Tallahassee, Fla.

Foote, Shelby. *The Civil War: A Narrative, Fort Sumpter to Perryville.* Vol. 2. New York: Random House, 1958.

Forst, Lee. "FWB Built on Sound Foundation." In *Our Town.* Fort Walton Beach, Fla.: Northwest Florida Daily News, 1992.

Fotheringham, Nick, and Susan Brunenmeister. *Beachcomber's Guide to Gulf Coast Marine Life: Florida, Alabama, Mississippi, Louisiana, and Texas.* Houston: Gulf Publishing, 1989.

Gannon, Michael. *Florida: A Short History*. Gainesville: University Press of Florida, 1993.

Gilman, J. H. "With Slemmer in Pensacola Harbor." In *Battles and Leaders of the Civil War: The Opening Battles*, ed. by Robert Underwood Johnson and Clarence Clough Buell. Secaucus, N.J.: Castle, 1991.

Golden, Pam. "Prosperity, Fame, Disaster Part of Tale of Okaloosa's Hub City." In *Our Town*. Fort Walton Beach, Fla.: Northwest Florida Daily News, 1992.

Gore, Robert II. *The Gulf of Mexico*. Sarasota, Fla.: Pineapple Press, 1992.

Grayton Beach State Recreation Area. "Native Plants." (Pamphlet.) Florida Department of Environmental Protections, Tallahassee, Fla.

Griffing, Jane R. *Letters from Florida on the Scenery, Climate, Social and Material Conditions, and Practical Advantages of the "Land of Flowers."* Lancaster, N.H.: Printed at the Republican Office, 1883. Reprint, Louisville, Ky.: Lost Cause Press, 1965.

Hallenbeck, Cleve. *Álvar Núñez Cabeza de Vaca: The Journey and Route of the First European to Cross the Contintent of North America, 1534–1536*. Port Washington, N.Y.: Kennikat Press, 1970.

Hartman, Brad. "Plants." In *Rare and Endangered Bioto of Florida*, vol. 5, ed. Peter C. H. Pritchard. Gainesville: University Press of Florida, 1992.

Higham, Charles. *The Duchess of Windsor: The Secret Life*. New York: McGraw-Hill, 1988.

History of Walton County. (Pamphlet.) Walton-DeFuniak Springs Library archives.

"How Defuniak Springs Acquired Its Name." *Historical Society of Okaloosa and Walton Counties Newsletter* 4, no. 7, March 1973.

Hudson, Charles. *The Southeastern Indians*. Knoxville: University of Tennessee Press, 1976.

Hudson, Charles, Chester B. DePratter, and Marvin T. Smith, "Hernando de Soto's Expedition through the Southern United States." In *First Encounters: Spanish Explorations in the Caribbean and the United States, 1492–1570*, ed. Jerald T. Milanich and Susan Milbrath. Gainesville: University Presses of Florida, 1989.

Huettel, Wilfred "Chick." "Early Settlements around Hogtown Bayou."

Hutchinson, Leonard Patrick. *History of the Playground Area*. St. Petersburg, Fla.: Great Outdoors Publishing, 1961.

Huyck, Tom. "Communities Grew with Blueberry Industry." *Our Town*. Fort Walton Beach, Fla.: Northwest Florida Daily News, 1992.

Iberville, Pierre le Moyne d'. *Iberville's Gulf Journals*. Trans. and ed. Richebourg Gaillard McWilliams. Tuscaloosa: University of Alabama Press, 1981.

Junior Service League Fort Walton Beach. *Recollections*. Fort Walton Beach, Fla.: Junior Service League.

Kennedy, Stetson. *Palmetto Country*. Ed. by Erskine Caldwell. New York: Duell, Sloan and Pearce, 1942.

Kittredge, Frank Edward. *The Man with the Branded Hand*. Rochester, N.Y.: H. L. Wilson Printing, 1899.

Knight, Vernon James, Jr., ed. *The Moundville Expeditions of Clarence Bloomfield Moore*. Tuscaloosa: University of Alabama Press, 1996.

Lanier, Sidney. *Florida: Its Scenery, Climate, and History*. Philadelphia: J. B. Lippincott, 1876.

Lazarus, Yulee W. *The Buck Burial Mound.* Fort Walton Beach, Fla.: Temple Mound Museum, 1979.

———. *Indians of the Florida Panhandle.* Fort Walton Beach, Fla.: Temple Mound Museum, 1968.

Lockwood, C. C. *The Gulf Coast: Where Land Meets Sea.* Baton Rouge: Louisiana State University Press, 1984.

Massoni, Julie. *Camp Pinchot.* Office of History Armament Division Eglin Air Force Base, 1988.

McKinnon, John L. *History of Walton County.* 1911. Reprint, Gainesville, Fla.: Palmetto Books, 1968.

Mettee, Vivian Foster, and associates. *Destin History: . . . And the Roots Run Deep.* Destin, Fla.: Vivian Foster Mettee and Associates, 1970.

Milanich, Jerald T. *Archaeology of Precolumbian Florida.* Gainesville: University Press of Florida, 1994.

Milanich, Jerald T., and Susan Milbrath, ed. *First Encounters: Spanish Explorations in the Caribbean and the United States, 1492–1570,* ed. Jerald T. Milanich and Susan Milbrath. Gainesville: University Presses of Florida, 1989.

Mitchem, Jeffery M. "Sylvanus T. Walker's Adventures in Florida." Paper presented at the 52nd annual meeting of the Florida Anthropological Society, Fort Myers, May 6, 2000.

Myers, Ronald L., and John J. Ewel. eds. *Ecosystems of Florida.* Orlando: University of Central Florida Press, 1990.

National Geographic Society. *Wonders of the Ancient World.* National Geographic Atlas of Archaeology. Washington, D.C.: National Geographic Society, 1994.

Nature Trails: Fred Gannon Rocky Bayou State Recreation Area. (Brochure.) Tallahassee: Department of Environmental Protection.

Naval Live Oaks. (Brochure.) Gulf Islands National Seashore, National Park Service, [2000].

Naval Live Oaks Trail Guide. (Brochure.) Gulf Islands National Seashore, National Park Service, [2000].

Nelson, Gil. *Exploring Wild Northwest Florida.* Sarasota, Fla. Pineapple Press, 1995.

Newell, Jeff. "Florosa Gets Name from Inn." *Our Town.* Fort Walton Beach, Fla.: Northwest Florida Daily News, 1992.

Nicolson, Nigel. *Virginia Woolf.* New York: Viking, 2000.

Niering, William A. *Wetlands.* Audubon Society Nature Guides. New York: Knopf, 1985.

Norton, Charles Ledyard. *Handbook of Florida.* New York: Longmans, 1892.

Núñez Cabeza de Vaca, Álvar. *Cabeza de Vaca's Adventures in the Unknown Interior of America,* trans. Cyclone Covey. Reprint, Albuquerque: University of New Mexico Press, 1984.

Parks, Virginia. *Christmas in Old Pensacola.* Pensacola: Pensacola Historical Society, 1978.

———. *Pensacola: Spaniards to Space-Age.* Pensacola: Pensacola Historical Society, 1986.

Pearce, George F. *Pensacola during the Civil War: A Thorn in the Side of the Confederacy.* Gainesville: University Press of Florida, 2000.

Pensacola Historical Society. *The Golden Dream: Life in Pensacola in the 1870s.* Pensacola: Pensacola Historical Society, 1974.

Pickett, Albert James. *Letters from Pensacola, Descriptive and Historical (1858).* Pensacola: University of West Florida, John C. Pace Library. 1985.

———. *History of Alabama.* 1851. Reprint, Montgomery, Ala.: River City Publishing, 2003.

Pryor, William Columbia. "The Most Unforgettable Character I've Met: Portrait of a Fast-Disappearing Breed." *Reader's Digest,* December, 1955.

Ripple, Jeff. *Sea Turtles.* Stillwater, Minn.: Voyageur Press, 1996.

Rolfsen, Bruce. "Destin's Heritage Lies in Tradition of the Sea." *Our Town.* Fort Walton Beach, Fla.: Northwest Florida Daily News, 1992.

———. "Grayton Beach Stakes Its Claim as One of Area's Oldest Towns." *Our Town.* Fort Walton Beach, Fla.: Northwest Florida Daily News, 1992.

———. "Quiet Walton Hamlet Had Its Roots in Lumber." *Our Town.* Fort Walton Beach, Fla.: Northwest Florida Daily News, 1992.

Romans, Bernard. *A Concise Natural History of East and West Florida.* 1775. Reprint, New Orleans: Pelican, 1961.

Rucker, Brian R. "West Florida's Creek Indian Crisis of 1837." *Florida Historical Society: The Florida Quarterly* 69, no. 3, 1–17.

Sandestin: The Magazine of the Premier Resort on the Gulf Coast. Sandestin Golf and Beach Resort, 2005 edition.

Short, Payton. *Annual Report of the Historical and Philosophical Society of Ohio.* December 17, 1809.

Smith, Marvin T. "Indian Responses to European Contact: The Coosa Example." In *First Encounters: Spanish Explorations in the Caribbean and the United States, 1492–1570,* ed. Jerald T. Milanich and Susan Milbrath. Gainesville: University of Florida Press, 1989.

Smith, T. Buckingham, trans. Foreword to *Relation of Núñez Cabeza de Vaca,* by Álvar Núñez Cabeza de Vaca. Ann Arbor, Mich.: University Microfilms, 1966.

Smith, Tommy. *The History of Bay County: From the Beginning.* Panama City, Fla.: Bene/ Mac Publishing, 2000.

South Walton Tourist Development Council. *Beaches of South Walton.*

Stewart, Catharine L., and Maude Hollowell. *Old Customs of Pensacola and Favorite Recipes of the Times.* Pensacola: Pensacola Historic Preservation Society, 1974.

Sutton, Juanealya McCormick. *The Man behind the Scenes.* 1987.

Tapia, Milan. *Spanish Approach to Pensacola, 1689–1693.* Trans. Irving A. Leonard. Albuquerque, N.M. : Quivira Society, 1939.

Tebeau, Charlton W. *A History of Florida.* Coral Gables, Fla.: University of Miami Press, 1971.

Urquhart, Fred A. "Found at Last: The Monarch's Winter Home." *National Geographic* 150, no. 2 (August 1976): 161–73.

Van Andel, Tjeerd H. *Tales of an Old Ocean: Exploring the Deep-Sea World of the Geologist and Oceanographer.* New York: Norton, 1978.

Walker, Jonathan. *The Branded Hand: Trial and Imprisonment of Jonathan Walker.* New York: Arno Press, 1969.

Weber, Michael, Richard T. Townsend, and Rose Bierce. *Environmental Quality in the Gulf of Mexico: A Citizen's Guide.* Washington D.C.: Center for Marine Conservation, 1992.

Welcome to the Indian Temple Mound Museum. (Brochure.) Fort Walton Beach, Fla.: Indian Temple Mound Museum, [2000].

Wells, William James. *Pioneering in the Panhandle.* Fort Walton Beach, Fla.: Melvin Business Services, 1976.

Wenzel, Tracy. "Mail Left on Mary Esther." *Our Town.* Fort Walton Beach, Fla.: Northwest Florida Daily News, 1992.

Willey, Gordon R. *Archeology of the Florida Gulf Coast.* 1949. Reprint, Gainesville: University Press of Florida, 1998.

Windsor, Wallis. *The Heart Has Its Reasons.* New York: D. McKay, 1956.

Wolverton, Ruthe, and Walt Wolverton. *The National Seashores: The Complete Guide to America's Scenic Coastal Parks.* Boulder, Colo.: Roberts Rinehart, 1994.

Womack, Marlene. *Along the Bay: A Pictorial History of Bay County.* Norfolk, Va.: Pictorial Heritage Publishing, sponsored by Junior Service League of Panama City, 1994.

———. *The Bay Country of Northwest Florida.* Apalachicola, Fla.: New Hope Press, 1998. Wood, Virginia Steele. *Live Oaking: Southern Timber for Tall Ships.* Boston: Northeastern University Press, 1981.

Woodward, David. "The L&N and DeFuniak Springs." *Dixie Line.* Third quarter (1991): 4–9.

Ziewitz, Kathryn, and June Wiaz. *Green Empire: The St. Joe Company and the Remaking of Florida's Panhandle.* Gainesville: University Press of Florida, 2004.

Zimmer, Carl. "Monarch Butterflies." *Discover.* May 1996: 38, 39.

Index

Jean Lufkin Bouler is an award-winning reporter who worked at the *Birmingham News* for ten years, writing features and in-depth stories about education in Alabama. For twenty-five years, she has vacationed on the Emerald Coast.

Related-interest titles from University Press of Florida

Apalachicola River: An American Treasure
Clyde Butcher

Beyond the Theme Parks: Exploring Central Florida
Benjamin D. Brotemarkle

*Dream State: Eight Generations of Swamp Lawyers,
Conquistadors, Confederate Daughters, Banana
Republicans, and Other Florida Wildlife*
Diane Roberts

*Green Empire: The St. Joe Company and the Remaking
of Florida's Panhandle*
Kathryn Ziewitz and June Wiaz

Highway A1A: Florida At the Edge
Herbert L. Hiller

Key West: History of an Island of Dreams
Maureen Ogle

*Weeki Wachee, City of Mermaids: A History of One of
Florida's Oldest Roadside Attractions*
Lu Vickers and Sara Dionne

Michael Gannon's History of Florida in Forty Minutes
Michael Gannon

Saving South Beach
M. Barron Stofik

Seasons of Real Florida
Jeff Klinkenberg

Voices of the Apalachicola
Compiled and edited by Faith Eidse

Waters Less Traveled: Exploring Florida's Big Bend Coast
Doug Alderson

For more information on these and other books, visit
our Web site at www.upf.com.